Through It All

By Scott Adrian Boggs

Table of Contents

Introduction

On my Mother's side of the family we have always been told that we were related to Samuel Clemens. He is better known by his pen name Mark Twain. Perhaps writing is just something in my blood. One of Mark Twain's famous quotes states that the two most important days in a man's life is when he is born and the other, the day he discovers what he was born for.

Now, this could all just be another grandiose idea of mine, that will be discarded like many other scribbled thoughts and unfinished projects but either way, whether I can get through this successfully or not, I am going to give this unraveling and retelling of my life (thus far) a good honest attempt here.

I'm not sure if anything will come of this.

All I know is that right now, I am feeling very compelled to write a book, almost as if this is that second day of discovery for me.

Chapter One

Mother Mother

Both of my Mother's parents, Clarence and Ada, were born and raised in West Virginia where they both loved Jesus and music deeply. All of my relatives on my mom's side of the family seemed to have that inherited faith and bluegrass music gene. Growing up, my mom says that they would all gather around each other's homes and pick banjos, strum guitars, stomp their feet and sing old gospel hymns together. My Grandfather Clarence, when he was 16 years old, got to play a song he wrote on a popular television show called The Ted Mack Original Amature Hour. In the late 1940s that was a big deal for everyone around. As the winner of that episode for "best singer, songwriter", he even got to have his own record pressed with 2 original songs on it.

According to my mom, life was good and filled with a lot of warm, loving family memories until my Grandfather had to go to the war. Hitler had become a threat to the world and Clarence ended up fighting in the front line of WWII carrying a bazooka on his shoulder in The Battle of The Bulge.

My Grandfather was six and a half feet tall and my mom always said it's been believed that this is why they stuck him on the front line with a bazooka. Life was never to be the same after his return home from the war.

When he came home, he told the family stories of having to lay in an open field for days, pretending to be dead, as German soldiers with bayonets on their guns would stab lying wounded American soldiers. They would walk around making sure all of the Americans were dead and my Grandfather said that one wrong breath could have cost him his life.

There was also the story he told about a little French girl, who had befriended the members of his platoon, a cute little girl about the age of five and he told of how she would come visit them and how they all enjoyed talking to her and feeding her, until one day he saw her approaching in the distance, just before an incoming grenade came in and exploded her into pieces.

As I had mentioned earlier, after the war, my Grandfather was never the same.

At one point, he had what they called in his day a flashback followed by a nervous breakdown. Sitting in the front room one afternoon, he all of a sudden got this weird sort of glazed and scared look in his eyes and he started calling my mom, who was only 5 years old at the time, by the same name as that little French girl. He then took my mom with him up on the roof of their house and held her like he was protecting her from invading German troops. He held her close in his arms and refused to leave the roof. I asked my mom once if she was scared and she said genuinely "Oh no, not at all, there was nothing ever at all about my Father to have been afraid of." As the evening started moving in, my Grandmother obviously perplexed about what to do, had no other option but to call the police. So the town sheriff, with a bullhorn and a whole lot of other police officers came out, along with my Grandfather's sister and Father and eventually they were all able to convince Clarence that it was getting way too cold up there for Martha and told him that he needed to bring her down before she caught a cold. At this, he agreed against my mom's will and let her down. My mom says she held him tight around his legs and begged him not to let her down because she knew that they were going to take him away. He was then handcuffed, taken into custody and sent to live in a veteran's hospital.

Although he did make a few attempts at reintegrating back into society over the years, the pressures of everyday living always seemed to be too much for him. So sadly, he ended up living out the rest of his days in the hospital with other wounded soldiers. He remained there, my mom says, chain smoking cigarettes until the day he died. He was only 42 years old when he got pneumonia and then died of a sudden heart attack.

To hear my mom talk of the strong, loving man he was before and even after the war, it can't help but to reveal the longing she has always had to recapture his love and presence.

One story she likes to tell, is how she remembers her mom Ada, a tiny woman just over 5 feet tall, fussing and all upset over something in their kitchen and my tall grandfather picking her up straight off her feet over his head and while laughing, telling her how she was "Not to worry."

Another time, my mom recalls before his confinement, was when she (my mom) , jealous of her newborn brother, had decided she was going to run away from home. At 6 years old, she packed up a little lunch sack and a change of clothes and decided to wander out as far as she could along the creek bank behind their house. As evening began to come in, she sat down on a log to eat her packed lunch and noticed that hundreds of little ants had gotten into it. Heart broken, afraid, hungry, cold and alone she bowed her little head down into her hands and started to cry, when right then, like a miracle, her Father appeared next to her wrapping a warm jacket over her arms. She was so happy to see him. Ecstatic would be more the word and he asked her "Are you ready to come home yet?" Unbeknownst to her, he had been following her in WWII soldier stealth mode the whole time and he told her that both her mom and him loved her just as much as they loved her new little brother and how although he may not always be around to keep his eyes on her, that God's eyes would always be watching over her and that God would always be there when she needed him.

From all accounts of family and friends, I have never heard a negative thing said about my Grandfather. He was described by others as a "Gentle Giant" who loved Jesus and in so many ways, just as the war had wounded and changed him, I believe his nervous breakdown and confinement after the war, as well, wounded and changed my mom.

The casualties of war travel far beyond the slain in the fields.

My Grandmother Ada was left dirt poor with 2 kids to raise and provide for in West Virginia, where work was scarce. After losing their home, moving in with her own mom seemed reasonable but unfortunately, there was an uncle on the property who had a reputation for putting his hands in places he shouldn't.

Sometime later, as I mentioned earlier, Clarence did come home from the hospital and worked for a time and they were even able to save up enough money to rent a small house together as a family again but eventually the P.T.S.D. would overtake him and he would have to return to the V.A. hospital. To treat him in those days, they would administer shock treatments.

My mom and her baby brother ended up moving back in at my Great Grandmother's house with that sick uncle. At 11 years old, while my mom was in the basement playing with her barbie dolls, he came down stairs and made a very inappropriate move on my mom, placing his hands on her breasts and commenting on how much she had been developing. My mom says she knew then that this was not going to be a good place to be living. One morning, not long after, she woke up with him standing over her fondling her and telling her that she'd better be quiet or he'd kill her Mother. No sooner than these ugly things began, my mom got herself and her baby brother out of the house and down the street to the local hardware store to call Izetta, her dad's sister.

My mom's Grandma said all of my mom's allegations about her son were false, my Great Aunt Izetta on the other hand, with some stern authority and perhaps even knowing, said to the family "give me that girl."

So my mom ended up staying with Izetta for three months, giving my Grandmother Ada enough time to save again for a place of their own.

Ada found a job with the local dry cleaners and was a faithful, hardworking, committed employee. Times were hard for Ada but once she got my mom and her little brother into another rented home again, my mom says times were good. The stories of their poverty and how they would ration food and equally share everything in the house is a true testimony of love and how to make the best out of what little one may have. My mom has warm memories of her and her mom and brother laying up late at night giggling and laughing together. They were poor but they were together and they were happy.

Growing up poor, my mom and Grandmother began attending a small pentecostal church up there in the hills of St. Albans, West Virginia. She recalls seeing many different tent revivals and faith healers that would come into town, pitch a tent, do a revival and then go. Being estranged from her own Father at this time, my mom developed a healthy love and respect for another male role model in the community known as Pastor Rogers. She tells the story of how he would come and pick her and her best friend Brenda up for church every Sunday and how even if she tried to play sick and stay home, he would come into the house and talk her into going anyways. With some church family, some love and a little fellowship, she began to get acclimated. She was reintroduced to some stability and began making friends at church and school.

She, like so many other kids growing up in the 50's and 60's, loved Elvis, going to sock hops and wearing skin tight, white jeans or "Hotpants" as she called them. She laughs when telling the story of how her and Brenda would have to lay on a bed and literally use pliers to zip each other's pants up. She'll laugh even harder when telling you the story of running down the side of a bridge and getting their brand new white pants all dirty, trying to hide from a car that they thought might be Pastor Rogers.

As a teen, she as well, became quite the soprano singer at church. As a kid myself, many years later, I can recall her singing louder than a whole Church and the choir from the pews we were sitting in. As gifted and powerful as her voice was, this honestly always made me want to hide under my chair. Similar to her dad's own achievement on tv in the 40's, when my mom was only 15 years old, she had won best soprano, all county and all state and got to do a duet on television with a young up and coming country and western star named Willie Nelson. Yep, The Willie Nelson! At that time, he was apparently a clean cut young man with a strong southern slur and soft strum. My mom became the talk around town as "The Girl That Sang With Willie Nelson."

Chapter Two

Father Father

My Father's parents, Adrian and Beulah, lived in St. Albans, as well. My dad did more of the farm life with his 4 siblings: Steve, Norman, Becky and Darlene. They even had their own well for water. I guess my Grandfather (Adrian) had bought into a lot of that Armageddon, end of the world stuff and was preparing his family for it. Ready and waiting for when it would all come down, he even bought a couple acres of land across the country in New Mexico, getting ready for their flight, if need be.

For many in those days, the belief was and still is for some that the end is near.

My dad apparently had to figure a lot of things out on his own as a kid. If he wanted something, he had to get out there and find a way to earn it for himself. As a young man, he used to caddy and once even caddied for Sam Sneed, a golfer known for winning 82 PGA tournaments. One day, after being out there on the green, Mr. Sneed gave my dad a hundred dollar tip and in those days that was a lot of money to a kid in St. Albans West Virginia.

My Grandfather on my dad's side was a deacon in The Church of The Nazarene before getting into a lot of the new age teachings that the church in St. Albans was not going to embrace. It was ultimately because of his continued interest in these "occultic things", that The Church would eventually see him as a lost, wayward heretic.

As a matter of fact, by the time my Mother and Father met, courted and decided to marry, the pentecostal town preacher (Pastor Rogers) made it clear to my mom, that he wouldn't marry my mom and dad, because my dad and his family were not believing, Christ confessing Christians. It wasn't long after, with my Grandmother Aida's blessing that my mom and dad decided to marry anyway. My mom at 15 years old and my dad at 18 were joined together in holy matrimony.

My Grandfather, Adrian Boggs, who had recently departed from the Christian Faith of the Nazarenes, jumped head over heels into the new age, metaphysics movement of the 1960's and ended up settling himself into one of those movements, later sects, called Eckankar.

It seems that my Grandfather, was really interested in things like dreams, interpretations of dreams, mind over matter, reincarnation and astral projection. All things that were being rejected and deemed by the Christian community as evil.

My dad recalls his Father as being quite distant and not much of a hands on kind of dad and although him and all of his siblings had a deep love and respect for his spirituality, I don't believe his attention and approval was ever really awarded or felt much by my Father. This could be that my dad was a middle child, who may have felt overlooked or even at times forgotten.

I believe this also may be why he has pursued so wholeheartedly his Father's religion. Perhaps in some ways, it's been to get closer and to somehow find and understand his Father.

With all love and respect for my dad, I do have issues with the spiritual path that my dad and at least two of his other siblings have chosen. It's where this path inevitably ends up taking it's followers. It takes them to Missouri, once a year on a trip to worship in a temple called a Ziggurat, also known as the worship sites of Babylonian and Assyrian gods, to chant to an entity named Mahanta.

I know it all sounds really strange if you haven't been exposed to stuff like this before, so to make a long story short, my Father prays and seeks guidance from what his religion calls "Ascended Masters" and it has been my own personal research, study and discernment that has revealed to me these "spirit guides" as nothing more than cunning, deceptive spirits, drawing their followers further and further away from the real love and connection that God Our Father wants us all to know and have with himself and one another.

Now, as I do believe in Angels sent to help us and minister to us along our often broken and lost ways, I as well, know the importance to be able to discern between the messengers that are sent to us from God and those that are not.

I believe it is also very plausible to say that my Father, just like my Mother, who did not have the love and presence of an involved Father in their life, may be suffering a life lived longing for this... A Father's Presence, that neither of them ever really got to fully experience... or at least on that healthy connected level, that every child truly longs for.

As a Christian, with all of my faith in Christ Jesus, I can see and say clearly that my Father's belief system is deeply rooted in paganism and it's origins come from founders, who have publicly confessed luciferianism to be at its core. So no matter how hard they try to hide or masquerade it, there is in fact, an agenda with this new age sect to try and deconvert Christians and convert them to be followers of a pagan entity.

Almost needless to say and as you could probably imagine, these two contrasting and often clashing religious points of view between my mom and dad, my mom being a Christian and my dad being a Pagan, would later make for me and my brother a pretty interesting and unorthodox upbringing.

I can vividly remember at 5 years of age, my mom wanting us all as a family to go to a Christian Church, here in our hometown of Bridgeview IL, while my dad's sister was sitting us down to read me and my brother's palms. I can recall my mom wanting to have friends from church over and my dad having my brother and I around a kitchen table, trying to bend forks with our minds. It was a childhood that taught me to be open, to say the least.

Interestingly enough, despite Adrian's departure from the Christian faith, he and my dad Perry actually come from a long lineage of what our ancestry calls Church Affiliated Individuals. One relative being a famous evangelist named David Livingston, was a man known for bringing The Gospel of Jesus Christ to the continent of Africa. A man so loved by the African people that it is noted in history that the natives had walked and carried his body over 1500 miles across the continent to give him a proper burial at sea.

My Father's last name "Boggs", became the surname, our ancestors took after we were exiled from Scotland to The Bogs of Ireland. The Bogs are swamplands that separate Northern and Southern Ireland. Prior to our surname, we were known as "The Livingstons", also known as "The Tribe of The King, The Tribe of The Priest." My Father's blood has a strong Christian lineage that can be traced all the way back to the ancient, Holy City of Ephesus. We are also related to the 37th King of High Ireland and as well to St. Moluag, a famous Scottish evangelist, known for bringing The Gospel of Jesus Christ to the indigenous people of Scotland, natives who were known as The Picts of Scotland.

All of this is why I also like to tell people that I have the most Scot Irish name you will ever hear. Scott Boggs. It doesn't get much more Scot Irish than that.

Eventually, my mom's English Heritage and my Father's Scot Irish blood would meet deep in the foothills of the Appalachian Mountains.

Shortly after marrying my Mother, my Father came to Chicago in search for work as a heat treater, a trade he had learned back home in St. Albans and once he found and secured a job and an apartment for himself, he sent for my now 17 year old mom. I have heard stories about my parents being so poor at this time, that one day my dad opened his lunch pail at work and found a peanut butter and jelly sandwich with a big bite taken out of. This story always makes my mom laugh when told about the early days of their financially struggling marriage.

Money and faith, just like in many marriages, actually became real serious issues and later reasons for great conflict in our family and home. The next chapter will shine a little light on just how dark and violent things unagreed upon, can actually become.

Chapter Three

What's going on

By the time I was born, my Father had landed a night shift job on 63rd St. in Chicago, as a heat treater for a company named Borg Warner and my Mother had worked her way up to a management position of a well-to-do clothing line store named Learners, at Ford City Mall. By this time, they had already given birth to my older brother Mark and although financially they had more now than when they had begun, more money in our home just meant more problems.

In a nutshell and with no holds barred, I was born into an extremely violent and scary, dysfunctional home life. By the time I hit the scene, there was a lot of traumatizing, rage-filled screaming and violent outbreaks going on between my mom and dad on a regular basis. Maddening screams from my frantic Mother, followed by loud growling rebuttals from my angry Father and a lot of slammed doors, shattered glass and emotional instability that blanket my mind's earliest childhood recollections. It was truly frightening.

I was born into a relationship between two people, that I guess at one time was filled with some sort of love and respect. Unfortunately, as a child I can't recall any of that though. How exactly my Mother and Father's love (worthy of marriage) had descended into what it had become, was a mystery to me. How their hate for one another had escalated into all of that rage, my brother and I had to continually endure, I believe would have to be more their story to tell.

Almost needless to say, all of the frequent outbreaks of rage caused for me and my brother a very emotionally unstable upbringing. The term "living on pins and needles", actually makes perfect sense to me. Much of this could have also played a small part and precursor to my teenage and young adult years strung out on heroin. I'm not saying this to blame anyone for my years of poor choices, I can't blame them for me but to deny the issues that I was self-medicating, would be to not tell the whole truth either. I will get more into all of that later but let me stay here at the beginning for now.

My earliest childhood memories are of being home alone a lot, while my Mother worked and my Father slept. My dad worked the night shift from 11:00 at night till 7:00 in the morning. He worked all night and slept all day. He slept while my mom worked, many daytime and evening hours. Sometimes I wouldn't see her come home until well after dark. My older brother, who was 8 years older than me, would be in school during the day and I can remember lying in a crib crying and to my dad's amazement can even tell you what room and under what window my crib was. I remember my dad peeking in on me from time to time and me wanting him to pick me up and hold me so bad but as I quieted just seeing him there, he would then walk away and return to his room to sleep. Not much would change to my knowing for the next couple years, except that I would eventually grow big enough to climb out of my crib and explore the big empty house. While he slept, I can remember standing by our kitchen and bathroom sinks, wondering how long it would be before I could reach the water spickets.

As a child, I did a lot of musing and playing make believe. I did a lot of fighting imaginary bad guys and was always ready to conquer any intruders or enemies that might try to invade our home. I can remember walking down the hall, through our kitchen and into our family room, scared and alone but always committed to being strong and brave. I remember one time, even making up this whole elaborate story, of how a tall skinny man and a short fat man, wearing ski masks, were in our family room going through my dad's desk while he slept. I told my mom that evening when she got home, that they had climbed out of our front room window, before speeding away on black motorcycles.

At 5 years old, I had become quite the storyteller. I imagined this whole thing up in my head and told it to the family. I remember standing there with my mom and the Bridgeview Police, explaining to two officers what these motorcycle riding bandits looked like when one of the officers calmly and deliberately asked me: "Why would they have climbed out this small window here, why wouldn't they have just used this door when fleeing?" At 5 years old, obviously not wanting to get caught in a lie, I just kept silent and shrugged my shoulders. It's crazy what an overactive imagination and some loneliness can do to a kid wanting some attention. Not to mention, the imaginary friend I had created to keep myself entertained as well. I named him "Hot Scott" and I liked to blame things on him, like the day I spilled milk at our kitchen table. I believe in hindsight, that he was just some sort of way for me to psychologically combat so many hours of being left alone in an empty house. I can remember imagining "Hot Scott" standing outside my bedroom window by a lamp post while we all slept. Then he would come in the house with me to play during the day while my dad slept.

As I got a little older, there were times I would wake up and hear my dad in the bathroom across the hall getting ready for work. One of my greatest memories of my dad before the divorce, was him taking a few minutes after shaving one night and reading to me "Horton Hears A

Who." I will never forget that night and the smell of my dad's white T-shirt and his Old English cologne next to me while he read. Not many other times in my life had I felt so safe and loved. There is something about being a child under their Father's arm or on their Mother's hip, that I believe was designed by God and given to us to fulfill his plan for healthy homes, love and connection here on earth.

At about this same age, I can recollect my dad telling me to get in the car, because I was going to preschool and I don't recall any preparation speech or explanation up to this point. I just remember being scared, crawling behind a recliner and crying because I really didn't want to go. I mean really, really not wanting to go. I was very upset and can remember not understanding anything they were talking about at preschool. The teacher gave me a paper with circles and words on it, that I could not read or understand and I sat there my first day tapping probably a hundred purple dots with my crayon all over my paper. I was so lost and confused about what it was I was supposed to be doing with this crayon and these circles with letters in them and then all of a sudden it all just clicked for me. I remember, I was able to match the letters in the circle with the letters on the crayons and that was it. In my mind, I had learned all I had ever needed to know in preschool that year.

During recess, I remember grabbing a toy truck and wanting to go off and play by myself (as I was accustomed to), but some other kid with friends came and took it from me and began playing with it on the other side of the room. I was sad about this but I wouldn't cry. I stood strong. Then this little girl named Rosie came up to me and said "Hey, do you want to play house?" She started to cook me breakfast with plastic pots and pans and pour me some invisible tea. She was like an angel sent to me and I was feeling much better about this whole rude and awkward situation I had been thrown into by my dad. This is when that same mean little boy who stole my truck, laughed at me from across the room and began to make fun of me for playing with girls. I believe this may have been the day I decided to hate school. I can't lie. I never liked going to school. I have always been painfully introverted and shy. Throughout my school years, if I could have submerged into the walls to have not been seen, I would have.

When I wasn't in school feeling like a fish in the wrong pond and my Mother and Father weren't at home fighting with each other, I spent most of the summer months in the house with my older brother and all of his Rock-N-Roll friends. This was a whole other strange season in my young life. While mom and dad worked, I was being babysat by teenage potheads. It was a trip to say the least. My brother and his friends at the time had created a pretty popular garageband and had even got a call back audition to be on a pretty popular Saturday morning t.v. show, called "Kidding Around", a show that put young talented acts on the air. Against my dad's suggestion to do a Beatles song, they stayed true to their rocking roots and went with AC/DC. Unfortunately, the producers said that the material was a little too mature for their demographic and age group. My brother and his friends were all like 13 and 14 years old and the show was catering to that same age. They were really good on their instruments though and played some shows around town, like at the Bridgeview Park District building and had even got to do some outdoor events in our community. They made the local newspaper and were being praised by many for being so young and talented. What many in the neighborhood may not have known, was just how much these garageband kids who called themselves "Transformer" were starting to emulate their Rock-N-Roll Idols and how much partying they were all getting into.

While both my parents worked a lot of hours, I was being raised in an unsupervised house with kids who liked to drink, smoke pot, drop acid, huff scotch guard and make out with neighborhood girls. All of this would be going on in between practicing Kiss and Alice Cooper songs out in the garage. It was crazy. I mean, it was sort of like a Def Leppard after party going on at our house while mom and dad were off at work. A lot like That 70's Show, except with a lot less parental guidance and a lot more bad language, sex and drugs.

I was 5 years old and I guess teaching me to swear and giving me cigarettes was a way for my brother's friends to keep themselves amused. I remember one of my brother's friends lighting a cigarette off the kitchen stove and giving it to me right before I went off down the street on my bike to my friend's house. Needless to say, the day I knocked on my friend's door with a lit cigarette in my hand asking his mom if he could come out and play, he apparently wasn't allowed to hang out with me anymore... I went home and I was really upset about this and one of my brother's friends (whose father called Dead Weight) said to me "Forget about it. That kid was a fag anyways." So later on that week, the way I had internalized and reacted to this whole traumatic event of losing my friend, was to stand up on the school bus, call him a fag and kick him in his chest. He looked at me all shocked and confused and then I emotionally cut him off and out of my life forever.

I was 5 years old. I was hurt. I just lost my friend and the only explanation given to me was that he was a fag. I didn't even know what a fag was. I couldn't put two and two together and see that it was most likely the smoking that did this to me. I had no parental guidance to help me understand any of this. To me, at that age, fags were bad and cigarettes were good.

So here I am now, with no friends, stuck in a house full of teenage drug addicts who had chosen to make me their daily intoxicated amusement. I remember this stoner kid picking me up and sitting me on top of the bathroom door one day and asking me "Do you like it up there?" I said "yeah." Then he walked out and slammed the door shut behind him, pinching my butt like you wouldn't believe and leaving me to slam down on the hard floor below. It hurt and it winded me, they found these kinds of things funny. They torched my favorite Mork doll (from Mork and Mindy) and lit my Tonka Truck on fire. They would hold me down and lower long, dangling hockers of spit over my face, sucking them back up just before they'd hit my face. Once, my brother's friends stripped me naked in my parent's pool and wouldn't give me my clothes or let me back in the house until I agreed to walk out to the street and get the mail. While I was on my way to the mailbox, they called a teenage girl (that I thought was pretty) and told her "Get over here quick! It's an emergency!" As she came running from her house across the street to see what was going on, I was caught like a deer in the headlights, butt naked and frantic with nowhere to hide. I tried grabbing a small cushion off the porch swing to cover my privates but it wasn't big enough to cover my backside. I was so embarrassed standing there all hunched over and naked but felt vindicated when she started scolding all of them for being so mean to me. They just laughed and laughed....

At this time, in my young life it wasn't unusual for me to walk around my house and see a lot of smoke and kids making out. I can remember hearing "Hell's Bells" a popular song at the time from AC/DC pounding out of our 8 track house stereo with 3 foot speakers, seeing my brother lying on top of a girl with his hand down her pants moaning and telling her how much he wanted her. Him and his friends would draw crude, inappropriate things on the rafters in our garage and everything you can imagine from cucumbers to mic stands became things they could stick between their legs and joke about having huge penises. I mean this stuff in my childhood was like Spinal Tap, the pre-teen years, for me during my most formative years.

Around this same age, I can remember being picked up by this teenage girl, who I thought was beautiful. She cradled me in her arms like a little baby, which I was. I remember how nice it felt to be picked up and held like a baby. I don't recall much of that as a child. It was comfortable and it felt really nice but then she began to sensually kiss me, the way I saw these girls kissing the older boys. "Not bad," I thought to myself for a 5 year old to be kissing a 15 year old. At least that's what I remember thinking. My brother's friends were all laughing, drinking and smoking in our driveway while this older girl instructed me and taught me how to "use more tongue."

Later on that evening, when everyone had gone home and it was just me and my brother standing around, I told him that I thought I might be in love with her and he just called me "Stupid" and walked away.

In hindsight, I think he might have been jealous.

My brother was only 15 years old at the time and when him and his friends weren't partying in our unsupervised house and garage, my parents would be home from work starting another emotional WWIII in the house.

I can remember hiding at a neighbor's house across the street, hearing our screen door being slammed and words like "You Crazy Bitch" being screamed at my Mother while she frantically cried and shrieked. She did this a lot, as if my Father was murdering her or something.

The neighborhood must have grown somewhat used to these kinds of outbursts coming from our house and to me, it was just how it was.

Chapter Four

Stop in The Name of Love

At this age, I'd developed what I believe was a defense mechanism which enables me to block out everything that's going on all around me. Even to this day, I can sit in a crowded room "stuck in my own little world", a default of character I still struggle with even as an adult.

I remember one night sitting in my bedroom while my parents were fighting. I sat there all by myself crying in the corner, hoping one of them would stop and notice me, notice that I was hurting while they were doing this to each other when I *realized* that their hatred toward each other seemed to be more important to them than any real love or concern either of them seemed to really have for me.

So at a very young age, I developed this attitude that I didn't really need them anymore. What I figured I needed to do was to become fiercely independent.

I decided that I didn't really need them or anyone for that matter anymore.

A lie that I wasn't really loved or cared about took deep root in my heart that day and I would end up carrying this lie with me for many years to come.

I can remember this same particular evening, as they continued their screaming up and down the hallway that night, being the same evening that I had learned how to escape into my new found love and adoration for music.

Up until this point, I would just drift off into my own imagination to escape neglect or their loud, frightening outbursts but this evening I had found another place to go in my mind and this place had a soundtrack to go along with it.

I remember sitting in the corner of my bedroom on the floor crying and after I had no more tears left... I turned on a little radio I had sitting there in my room and to my amazement found that I could magically point my finger every time the snare drum would hit. I mean, this was like awakening some sort of mystical power to me. I couldn't believe how amazing this was. I could point my finger at the same time that snare drum would go "snap" and I was really good at it. I could predict it and nail it perfectly every time. It was something that I was able to control and it gave me a sense of peace in the midst of what seemed like such uncontrollable chaotic circumstances. The beat gave me a steady sense of comfort and predictable peace. It didn't even matter to me anymore, as my mom and dad continued their rampage up and down the hallway that night.

I had now finally found a way to take flight and soar above all of that nerve wrecking, mind shattering madness.

What I had found was rhythm. A gift, I believe God gave me to center me and even still to this day, whenever I am near a drum set, I can go into a trance like state on them. I'm not saying that I am the greatest drummer or musician in the world or anything like that because I'm not. I'm not even a trained musician... Whether it has been on drums, piano, bass or guitar, I have always played by ear and my skills on instruments are very limited compared to many others but nonetheless, I can definitely find comfort while pouring my soul out on a drum kit, while playing keys or picking strings. It's all very therapeutic for me.

At a very young age, words and music became an amazing blessing in my life.

They were given to me like a lifeline.

Before I go on, I would like to share with you a poem I wrote about 8 years ago, concerning the very night I found rhythm... while crying in that corner as a kid.

Stop

"I must confess this mess, and all the years I have been here, all withdrawn and isolated, another step further away, each time others would try and draw near, rejection and busyness, anxiety and fear, words being yelled and thrown at one another like spears... Becoming more and more inattentive, with these stopped up ears, not even able to hear. Seeking comfort in books and quotes, online posts, unconnected from family and friends, a depression that will take heavenly hosts... While left all alone in here, in my own little world. Crying out to no one, in this long hallway, hoping they'd just STOP and notice my tears... STOP all the yelling and screaming and show me they care. Show me that they can see that I'm hurting and that I'm confused and that I'm scared... All I hear anymore is more fighting and yelling, year after year, after year... Hiding in a corner, seeking comfort from a snare... That consistency on the radio that I heard and that I could rely on, that beat leading those songs on and from then on, I always knew that I could just go there, timing my words and humming in my mind, these melodies, these rhythms, these rhymes and beating on my chest to the passion of these songs, knowing when to refrain and when to go on... When to go soft and when to go strong... The Pen, The Paper and these songs, I would ponder on and on and on... Expressing myself in rhythms and words, this gift I

*had stumbled upon, opening finally some sense of comfort, peace and purpose to me. Somewhere between poetry and song, like The Psalms, this is where I found you Lord. My true safe place, my peace, my comfort, my faith and my strength, away from my mom and dad's arms... I found you God, to express from deep down inside what was really going on... And after all... I guess I'm still a little confused, scared and hurt while the whole world just keeps going on and on and on... At times, in the hope of peace and at times in the waging of war, whether nations are dancing and twirling around together in love or raising their voices, clashing shields and banging their swords.... I still at times feel like that scared little child in my room full of dreams and broken toys, just wanting the whole world to STOP... For us all to just STOP and notice each other's broken and frightened hearts... **I guess this is where it all must have start..** Their own rejection and busyness, their own anxiety and fear. Their own pain and plan of escape from here to there. Their own mess... my neglect... I must confess... Oh Father God, who art in heaven... hallowed be your name and to all who hear and do care... Can you make it all STOP... so we can notice the ones who are still hurting here? I'm wanting it all to Stop and for someone to draw near... To draw near ... Not for pity... not for shame but for Real Love... God's Love, God's perfect love... that casts out all fear."*

Although, I have tried to write up to this point as lighthearted and comical about many of these childhood experiences here as I could, the truth be told, these kinds of things were years that did instill a lot of confusion and fear in me.

Depression, anxiety, low self esteem, anger, confusion and fear are ugly demons of the mind and soul that I have had to contend with spiritually my whole life. I have had a lot of issues that I tried to medicate with street drugs for many years. With the help of God and family, I can say today, that much needed deliverance and healing has taken place in my life.

I can only imagine how much more pain and fear my older brother Mark must have felt, as he witnessed 8 more years of this kind of childhood terror. The terror that was my mom and dad's violent fights. As a kid, he had even developed a nervous habit of chewing his fingernails off. Totally off. The whole thing off. He chewed them until they were completely gone. Talk about nervous habits. If you could only imagine the stress of his young heart and I had experienced living in the same house with my mom and dad.

You see, during our most formative years, my brother and I were molded and shaped around many traumatic and frightening events that left deep wounds in our soul and searing memories burned in our minds. As I write this, I can see a toaster shattering a glass mirror on the back of a bathroom door and a locked bedroom door slowly being picked open with a butcher knife to get into a room that me and one of my parents were trying to hide in. Memories of mind and wounds of soul that tormenting fears like to move into and take up residency in.

You see, often when we are at our most vulnerable points in life, this is when ugly fears will come along and begin to whisper lies to us, about us, about others and even about God Our Father, if we let them. If we are not taught and grounded firmly in the truth, especially as a kid, it can become pretty easy for us to fall for these lies and come into agreement with these mean allegations that come. Even worse, once we have come into agreement with these lies, it then gives them permission to stick around and hinder the growth and progression of our lives. The quality of our lives and our relationships with others can be stifled and hindered at best. Worry not though, these dark lies are nothing, once they have been brought out into the light. There is no lie, that the truth of God will not easily dispel. All of these lies that the devil likes to whisper to us when we are down and out and most vulnerable are destined in Christ to be exposed and dealt with by the light.

When for example, we turn our hearts to Jesus and like King David says similarly, in our own way and in our own words;

"Search me, O God, and know my heart; Try me and know my anxious thoughts; And see if there be any hurtful way in me, And lead me in the everlasting way." ~ Psalms 139:23:-24

I have come to find *"The Everlasting Way"* to be the way of God's love and forgiveness and this truly is where all of my healing and deliverance began.

As a Christian Minister I have known and spoken with so many people who have had their own traumatic events growing up as kids and it's never an issue of who has had it better or worse, whether one has been lied to, beaten, abused, neglected or raped...

As kids or adults, trauma is trauma and pain in us bleeds the same.

Please understand that there should never be any sort of competition here. I don't believe anyone should ever go into the demeaning of another who is presently suffering real emotional pain. Often, I have heard people rebuttal someone else's pain by decreeing an angry articulation of their own. I have been guilty of doing this myself. Telling someone that I have had it worse and that they just need to stop feeling sorry for themselves and toughen up. Though the rebuttal may say in a way "I can relate", I'm not sure that the mere acknowledgement of each other's pain, alone, is ever going to be enough to minister the real genuine healing of God in those deep, hurting, dark places. Those places we hide. Those places where those lies hide.

In these touchy areas of our own personal pain and wounding, it can all become quite irrelevant in the end and it's not as much about the events themselves, as much as it becomes more about the exposing of those lies that we have come to believe during those traumatic events.

Remember, "I was never really loved or cared about?"

  Let me deflect a bit more, for a moment here, to say that if at any time these recollections of my own life remind you of any resentments, judgements or unresolved pain and unforgiveness that you may be holding onto of your own. If at any point throughout the remainder of my story you are brought face to face with any lies you may have knowingly or unknowingly been believing about yourself, someone else or even God, if anything dark and unsettling begins to surface and rear it's ugly head, it is my prayer that even now, Father God, Jesus Christ, The Holy Spirit and Heaven's Angels will use this transparency that I am painstakingly writing with here, to expose and dispel these lies.

I pray that all who need to, will break their unhealthy agreements with lies and experience agreement with God's Powerful Truths about us and others and that the love of God that casts out all our unhealthy fears will prevail in my testimony, freeing and healing us and cleansing us all from deep down within.

Whenever you or me experience the surfacing of any unbalanced judgement, unforgiveness, bitterness, hurt, shame or rage coming up in our lives, I believe we need to first admit it and then upon that confession, welcome The Holy Spirit to work it out of our hearts, so that there can be room now for real love, healing and genuine forgiveness. If you are personally holding onto any unforgiveness in your life, perhaps from the mistakes of your own caretakers or neglect and abuse from a spouse or the rejection of a child, the dismissal from a job, the judgments of others or the ostracizing of a church and so on…

I ask Father God to search it out right now, to find it, identify it and let's allow The Holy Spirit and Heaven's

Hosts to dispel it, so we can experience God's love, forgiveness and healing power together.

Chapter Five

Teach Your Children Well

My parents eventually did divorce and my dad and brother moved away when I was 7 years old. I remember lying up late at night weeping tears into my pillow hoping my dad would change his mind and come back home. Before he moved out he sat me down and told me that he and my mom were having some problems and that he was going to be staying at a hotel for a few days but "Not to Worry" that I would see him again.

However long that season really was, it seemed like forever to me.

I was used to seeing my dad go to Dunkin Donuts (a local coffee joint) at night to avoid conflict with my mother. I also remember many nights, him creeping his car back home into our driveway and sleeping in his car.

After he left home, every car that came down the block at night, I would hope so earnestly for it to be my dad coming home. Every car, I remember standing on these little hot floorboard radiators and using my fingers to grab and pull myself up on the window ledge to see if it was him coming down the street. I remember wanting every car to be my dad so bad. I remember thinking "If he just pulls up in the driveway and sleeps in the car, that would be great!" I would grasp that window ledge with my little fingers and fight the heat on my feet as long as I could, hoping these cars would be my dad coming home. Sadly, none of the cars ever did turn into our driveway.

One night, while weeping his absence and crying into my pillow, an apparition appeared at the foot of my bed. It appeared to me as a shadow with a bright white light shining behind it and I heard a voice simply say "I Am Here." I used to think that was an Angel sent to comfort me but today I question it to have possibly been a fear of abandonment that came appearing as an angel of light because from that night on, I had developed a fear that God might leave me. I would pray and ask Jesus to stay with me every night and I'd refuse to say Amen because I was afraid that when I said Amen that Jesus would leave. I would tell Jesus "I will say Amen in the morning" because I was afraid and didn't want him to leave me like my dad did.

At a very young age, I began to believe *the lie* that God may leave me too.

As I had mentioned earlier on, when my dad had left he had taken my brother with him, so this made me what some like to call "a latchkey kid." That's a child who comes home after school and has to let their own self in. So one day, on a Friday after school, while my mom was at work and I was sitting in the house all alone again (a recurring theme of my life) and my dad shows up unexpectedly and it's one of the most exciting moments of my life! He came in through the front door and said to me "Hey, do you want to go swimming?" Of course I did. I said "Yes!" He said "I'll have you back by 5:30", so I called my mom at work and told her that my dad was there to take me swimming and that he would have me home by 5:30. She reluctantly said "ok" amidst my obvious joy and excitement. I was then taken to a local hotel where my dad told me that my stay with him was going to be until 5:30 on Sunday. I was elated to see my dad and brother again but very worried about what my mom would think when I wasn't home later that evening. According to my mom and her friend, I was later told that I was kidnapped and that they were panicking, calling and searching the whole world over for me. This is also when I got to meet my soon to be stepmother and her son. I can't honestly say that I was as excited and accepting about this one, it was all really so out of the blue for me. I was more confused and worried about how my emotional mom back home was going to feel about all of this.

You see, up until this point, all I remember was my mom crying and praying with me every night for my dad and brother to come back home.

After keeping me for the weekend, he safely returned me home that Sunday.

Shortly afterwards, a judge did grant my dad every other weekend visitations and one full month with me in the summer. He also ordered my dad to pay my now single mom bi-monthly child support checks. This was very helpful to me and mom. The courts as well contracted in their divorce papers that my mom and I could live in the house, as long as my mom could keep up the house payments until I was 18 but then she would have to sell the house and divide the profits with my dad and his new wife.

This was all very ugly and sad stuff for me as a child to witness. I was just a little kid who was really scared and confused and really wanted nothing more than for his mom and dad and brother to all be back home and together again.

At my first visit to my dad's new apartment, in the next town over, I was blindfolded and asked to lay down in the backseat of his car because he didn't want my mom to know where he and his new soon to be wife were going to be living. As I was sitting there in his "new place" trying to get used to all of this, I began to recognize the furniture. It was the furniture from my house.

Even that desk I was telling you about earlier that the ski mask wearing motorcycle bandits were going through!

After returning home to my mom's house that weekend, I found her sitting in front of a little 12 inch black and white t.v. crying in the middle of what used to be our family room. Now, it was just a big empty room. I remember it feeling cold to me but I don't believe it was because of the temperature. My mom got the house until I was 18 but it appears my dad and his new girlfriend got most of the family room furniture. It was all gone…. like our family.

At this point, I don't recall seeing my brother Mark much. The reason being is that after the divorce he had gone into a pretty bad downward spiral of substance abuse. From what I understand, he was doing a lot of LSD and although he lived at my dad's, I didn't see him much. I remember going to my dad's on the weekends and seeing my (soon to be) step brother more. He was always wrestling with me and making the neighbors in the apartment below us mad. My dad and his new girlfriend had moved to a place called Sunset Lake in Justice IL that was literally 99% African American populated. The 1%

that wasn't would have been us. My best friend there was a kid named Solomon Jones and he was the blackest 8 year old I had ever seen. He was great! He wore a vinyl jacket and had this huge black afro like you'd see in a 70's sitcom. We would play football, G.I. Joe's and ride our bikes up and down the hallways of all the apartment complexes. We had discovered that if we rode our bikes really fast and then slammed on our brakes and swerved our handlebars back and forth we could leave these really long, black streaks that looked like snakes down all of the complexes' bright orange carpets.

It was also here in Sunset Lake that I smelled my first dead body. I guess someone had been dead and decaying in one of the apartments in the next building over for sometime and me and Solomon got to get a good whiff of that before they had found and removed the decomposing resident.

After returning home from my bi-monthly visitations with my dad, my mom would always cry and beg me for more information about my Father's new life and soon to be wife. She would go on and on asking me questions, prying me for whatever information she could get, wanting to know every detail of my visit.

She wanted to know if I really believed my dad loved her and if I really thought he'd never come back home. Meanwhile, at my dad's new apartment the new nickname I heard being used for my mom had become "The Witch", so I sort of knew in my heart of hearts that my dad didn't have any fond feelings at all for my mom anymore but because I didn't want to see her hurt anymore than what she already was, I would just keep telling her "I don't know mom."

She probably cried on me and my shoulder at this point as many times as I had cried into that pillow at night wanting the same thing...

Just wanting my dad and brother to come home.

I remember my mom crying and holding onto me and begging me to please not leave her too... to not leave her like they did... perhaps like her dad did.

I don't know exactly how to say the following in any other way but that as a 7 year old child, who had just witnessed all of the above and more, I was now about to be graced and held by God as I watched my mom have an all and all out nervous/mental and emotional breakdown. I witnessed so many unreasonable and senseless things that I will in honor and out of respect for my mom refrain from sharing them all. Just let me say this, my mom's own devils and perhaps the amount of pressure she was under enmeshed with all of the abandonment issues she had suffered as a kid and all the stress of having her husband and son pack up and walk out on us with no sense of remorse, regret or hope of return, sent my mom spiraling down into a deep hole of verbal, physical and emotional abuse that I had to endure. I believe it's suffice to say that I had now become the one she was going to scream and yell at in my dad's place.

Just to give you a glimpse, I recall being held in a corner and spit on while being slapped repeatedly over and over as my mom kept calling me Perry Jr., my Father's name. I recall one evening her lying on our kitchen floor with an empty prescription bottle in her hand, telling me she was going to die now and not allowing me to call anyone for help.

There are so many episodes, I witnessed as a child that I'm not even sure where to begin, as it all sort of loses chronological rhyme and reason for me at this point.

I am repeatedly called pathetic and stupid and even called a cock sucker at one point. I watch her lay face down in the middle of the street one night saying she wants to be run over and die. I witnessed things like her covering her ears and shouting at the top of her lungs before going into uncontrollable frantic crying, right into eerily speaking in a small child's voice, singing "Jesus loves me this I know."

All night frenzies of her storming in and out of my bedroom verbally and emotionally abusing me while I just had to sit there and take it. God forbid, if I was to get sad and cry. If I cried, I was mocked and called "little baby" and if I got angry, I was called "big boy" and slapped harder.

I remember one evening her throwing my clothes out the back door and yelling at me to "Get Out", the way she used to tell my Father to get out. It was dark out and she slammed and locked the door on me. So I walked up to the nearby park where we lived and a short time later I was found by spot lights on a squad car that brought me home. On the ride home, I got a calm, short lecture from the officer about how it was against the law for me to run away.

Meanwhile, on my every other weekend visits to my dad's house he would ask me "How's everything going at home?", but me not wanting to get my mom in any trouble, I would just always say "fine."

One day, while staying at my dad's for the weekend, I was sitting on a couch somewhere between asleep and awake and I dreamed I was running through a field of high grass that turned into the front yard of my mom's house and as I ran up to the door and tried to turn the handle it was locked and extremely startled I woke up yelling "MOM". Later that evening, after sharing this story with her, she told me that at that same moment in time she was driving on the expressway not wanting to live anymore and she had closed her eyes and took her hands off the steering wheel but right before going off the side of the road she heard my voice yell "Mom" and it startled her enough to open her eyes and quickly regain control of the car.

A kind Christian woman who lived 2 doors down graciously took me in for a short time while my mom was hospitalized and treated for her mental/emotional health. After her return, this same neighbor invited us to attend church with her and her family.

It was a pentecostal church just like the one my mom grew up singing in as a kid in West Virginia. Our neighbor also helped my mom find a much needed new minimum wage job, answering phones at a local boy scout office. My mom always said she needed a job with a phone so she could easily be accessed by me.

All of this together brought a time of fresh renewal and hope to our broken home and situation. My mom's commitment to the services, her new job at the boy scout office and listening to Mike Kellogg on Moody Bible Institute (Chicago Christian Radio Broadcast) every night radically began a transformation in my mom's health and life that I was radically grateful for.

My mom's return to worship and her childhood faith and her hanging on to Jesus like he was the only thing she had left on this earth, for me was very influential. Watching my mom learning how to laugh again and for her to find some sort of peace in life and me knowing it was all because of her faith and obsession with this Christ. This was all very instrumental in my own decision to ask Jesus into my heart to be my own Lord and Savior.

Before The Stone Church became a part of our life, things had spiraled so far down and into such manic depression and madness that hope seemed almost obsolete to me. By this time, I'm not sure if my mom even knew what hope was anymore. Hope had long been shattered the day we'd both realized that my dad and brother weren't going to be coming back.

In so many ways, The Stone Church introduced hope and life to us all over again. The Stone Church had become like a pillar of hope. The people at Church seemed really kind and nice and the preacher was always talking about this Jesus who apparently had the ability to help us all through anything we were going through.

I remember asking my mom if I could be baptized? She asked The Pastor and he said "Yes". I was 9 now and I remember wearing my cross necklace and a pair of camouflage pants for the ceremony because I wanted to be a soldier for Christ.

On the way home that evening, my mom and I were driving over a bridge in our hometown of Bridgeview and I remember saying "Mom, I feel so clean."

She said "Well of course you do honey, you were just in the water",

and I said "No mom, I mean clean on the inside."

Our time at The Stone Church was tide turning to say the least. I remember a simple message written on a church bulletin from Pastor Phillip Epperson given to my mom one day that simply said "Hang in there Martha."

These words written by The Man of God hung on our refrigerator for years to come and always gave sustaining hope to me, in what had now become our slowly falling apart home. Literally, falling apart home.

Chapter Six

Blowin in The Wind

Our carpets were soiled and stinky from all the cats and dogs we had. Although my mom had to work a lot, she always made sure I had plenty of pets to keep me from feeling lonely. Holes had started to develop in our kitchen floor beneath our leaking washer and dryer and whenever stuff would break, it would just remain broken. There was no one around to fix it and at 9 and 10 years old I had no clue. By the time I had first learned how to fire up our lawn mower our backyard looked like a small Amazon Jungle. I was out there for 2 days trying to tackle that small rain forest of weeds and neck high grass. Then there was my mom's car. A Delta 88 Oldsmobile that was given to her by her brother in West Virginia that over time had developed holes in the floor and that we could see the street zooming past our feet as we drove. Still happy to have a working vehicle though, we would laugh and call it our Flintstones Car. One day, the whole driveshaft actually fell off the car while we were driving over another local bridge in our home town of Bridgeview.

I recall sleeping in the bed with my mom a lot and cuddling close to her to stay warm in the winter months as ice accumulated on the walls of our house. I remember stepping out of our bed and reaching out to the wood paneling on the walls and feeling nothing but ice and thanking God that my mom was so warm. The Christian neighbor after finding out about our situation had her husband come and teach me how to change a thermal coupling in our furnace and after that, we never had to freeze again. Over our remaining years there, I had to replace two of them.

I'm 10 now and I have already seen and experienced much of what the angels of madness could do to a person. I watched my mom helplessly as she descended into utter despair and depression and as well, I got to witness the hope of Jesus, my mom's resurrection and the true power of pentecost being poured out into our very broken situation.

My mom joined the kind neighbor's church for a season and I was put in a play called "Down By The Creek Bank." I had also become a "Royal Ranger" which was a lot like the christian cub scouts. A special thanks to Pastor John for getting me the uniform that my mom couldn't afford at the time. I even ended up going on an outing with the rangers that my dad had surprisingly agreed to go on with me and I can't even put into words how excited I was about this. I believe it was one of the only times just me and him had got to go do anything together, just me and him since the divorce. It was a canoe trip down The Fox River. He also came to see me sing in the kids choir that Christmas and at the end of the service when Pastor Epperson asked for every head to be bowed and for every eye to be closed, I peeked out from the stage to see if my dad was going to be one of the ones in the auditorium getting saved but he just sat there with his head up and his eyes wide open. Despite my hope, he didn't raise his hand or come forward. He still hasn't. Instead he has pursued his Father's new age path and has become a 5th initiate high priest in the religion of Eckankar where he conducts local services and can even marry people under their pagan god.

As for my brother and his relationship with Jesus, as a kid, I clearly remember him not wanting to go to church with my mom anymore. I guess one day at Sunday school in another differing church he had witnessed a screaming hand puppet being lit on fire and then doused with lighter fluid as a demonstration to the kids of what was going to happen to them if they didn't accept and love Jesus.

Yeah, so he never seemed very interested in Church too much after that.

He didn't seem really interested in much of anything spiritual my dad was wanting him to get involved with, either. So for him, life had pretty much become a steady pursuit of sex, drugs and rock n roll. His religion in many ways became Kiss, Led Zeppelin and The Who. He loved his guitar, his friends, getting drunk and wasted and he had this undying hope of making it as a famous rock star.

I had tried the kids Sunday school thing as well with my mom at The Stone Church but I, like my brother, had my own poor experience with that. The lady running the kids group (God Bless Her) sent us all home on a mission one week to remember a new bible verse. Normal Sunday school stuff. My verse was John 3:16 "For God so loved the world." The following week, I went back to Sunday school ready to recite my verse and I guess I had messed up somewhere along the way because I was denied a piece of candy. I was super let down over this and never wanted to go back but the backfiring good outcome of all of this was that I really became a lot better at remembering scriptures after that.

People have been telling me for years that I'm like a walking bible and I guess that would be partly true but not so much with the more commonly recited verses you hear from people. It has always been the verses that I could find on my own in The Bible and that spoke something directly and personally to me, that I could recall and recite. Not so much the ones someone else was telling me I had to remember. The ones I could find on my own, those verses I tend to remember and still to this day, I have a plethora of verses in my heart and mind that are not as common in other's arsenals.

So my mom saw how much not getting the candy upset me and so from then on she would let me go with her to "The Big Church." It was there that I got to listen to Pastor Epperson on much meatier and weightier topics. He would be teaching these deep biblical truths about The Holy Spirit, Power, Love, Life, Hope, Faith, and Forgiveness.

As he would go on about God's life changing Holy Spirit, I would always pray in my heart for my dad and my brother. One day, I even wrote Pastor Epperson a note and I stuck it in his hand after church asking him to please pray for my brother Mark who was on drugs. Many years later, as an adult I was blessed to speak with him on the phone one afternoon and the first thing he said to me was "How's Mark?"

He was a Real Pastor who really cared for his people.

Powerful messages and comforting seeds of Christ's words were sown into my little heart and mind every week. I was still very young, hurt, confused and greatly wounded but also very impressionable and I believe our stay with that ministry may have only been for a couple years but it was enough. This Church experience as a kid brought me and my mother some much needed hope, help, sanity and stability.

Four things in life I had known very little of.

Those sermons by Pastor Phillip Epperson sowed the incorruptible seed of God's Word into my young wounded heart and if there was any one impacting and lasting principle that I can remember taking with me from that whole amazing experience, sitting under pastoral care, it was undoubtedly the message conveyed for us all to "love the sinner but hate the sin."

It was that same message, that 20 years later would yield the fruit of my own breakaway and much needed deliverance and healing from many years of serious and life threatening substance abuse.

Chapter Seven

Kids in America

I am definitely an introvert at this point. I was a very quiet kid to say the least and I was known to keep to myself a lot. Back in elementary school they put me into some counseling sessions with the school psychiatrist. I remember her saying that I was very shy and showed signs of a photographic memory.

I pretty much did the bare minimum of what I needed to do in school and really couldn't wait to get home so I could watch The Flintstones and Brady Bunch. So one day while sitting at home alone after school, Mark (the drummer from my brother's old garage band) who in my mind was as good as Neil Peart from Rush, walked in the front door of our house and gave me his 5 piece, blue and glitter covered, vintage Slingerland drum kit.

That same afternoon, he taught me how to play "Rock-n-Roll All Night and Party Everyday" by the band Kiss and so from then on, for me, it was on like Donkey Kong. I was still alone every day after school but at least now I had these awesome drums to bang on between my Flintstones and Brady Bunch episodes.

In 5th grade, I remember coming home anxious to play the drums and deciding to stuff a failing report card down the sewer in front of my house. I can also remember thinking to myself how great it was that there was no one ever home to ask me about my homework or grades. This all seemed to be working out fine and in my favor. Coasting through grade school until the 7th grade came along and the teacher told me that I was going to have to be in what they called a special class. While all the other kids were going to start changing classes and getting their locker numbers assigned (The Joys of Junior High) they were saying that I was going to have to stay in one class room all day, with the same teacher. I was devastated. It made me feel like I was dumb or something. So my mom, as she always has, went to bat for me and begged the principal of the school to give me another shot with the other kids my age. She said she knew that I could keep my grades up if I were to try. She said that I just wasn't applying myself but that she knew I could keep up academically if I was just given the chance. You know what? She was right. They gave me the opportunity and in my first whole year of Junior High I scored in the high honors. They even took me on a field trip, where I got to meet the governor of Illinois in Springfield. I went from all D's and F's in 6th grade to all A's in Junior High but the truth is that I had to work hard at it. I had to do my homework and turn my assignments in on time. It may not have come as effortlessly to me as it may seem to come to others but a little effort took me a long way. I had to apply myself though. It's been the same in anything, I endeavour to do. Then or now. Applying myself. Something, I honestly sometimes still don't want to do.

All I wanted to do when I was 12 was get home and play the drums. I didn't want to work. I just wanted to bang on my drum all day. I had always reasoned to myself that 6 full hours of my day in school was enough time spent learning what they said I had to learn and I never wanted to go home and do more of their said learning. Home was where I wanted to learn what I wanted to learn and much of the time that was going to be a new drum track.

Let me say though that English and Music were strange exceptions for me. Those subjects always seemed to come with an anointing of ease for me. From very early on, I had this deep love and infatuation with words and music. I still do. Math and Science... not so much. Especially Math. I never liked math. Not since the day my dad got impatient with me and threw flash cards across the room. Yet, today as an adult, overseeing the administration of a religious organization, a thrift store and our own personal income, I probably use it just as much as anything else I use in this life… go figure.

So to make a long story a bit shorter here, after excelling in the 7th grade to prove that I could do as well as the other kids, I honestly got kind of distracted and bored and so by the end of the year, I found myself slacking a bit academically again and making friends with all these other underachievers and socially awkward outcasts who struggled as well. It's like we all just seemed to gravitate toward one another. If you had long hair, hated school and wore a metal t-shirt like me, you were now my friend.

My dad and his new family had moved from the African American apartment complex in Justice IL to a new home they had just bought about a half hour away in Evergreen Park. It was an exciting time for them and by now I had acclimated to my new step mom and brother. I actually even came to like my step mom quite a bit. She was always nice to me and seemed to go out of her way to try and connect. It didn't take much. A trip to see The Goonies in the 80's at the movie theater sealed the deal for me. I thought to myself, "She's alright."

The first friend I made in Evergreen Park was the neighbor's kid. We were the same age, in the same grade and the first time I met him he was lowering a cat in a basket tied to a rope from his second floor bedroom window to my dad's driveway. A couple weekends later he was taking me up on his roof, hitting golf balls as hard and far as he could and then listening intently into the distance for things to clang, bang or shatter. This was Mike and he was the same kid who ended up piercing my ear when I was 12, who made me my first screwdriver (vodka and orange juice) and reintroduced me to Marlboro's all over again. I was 12 years old now and it had been a good 7 years since I'd smoked my last cigarette.

I was friends with the kids in Bridgeview and in Evergreen Park that smoked, swore, wore black concert t-shirts, tried to get people to buy them beer (usually to no avail) and listened to really loud and fast heavy metal music. Many of us were poor and from homes that had been torn apart by things like drugs, alcohol, violence and divorce. In many ways, we were just emulating much of what we saw happening in our own homes with our own siblings and family members.

It has been said that children live what they learn… Right?

Nonetheless, we were the kids who had long hair, who weren't invited to much, probably not liked too much by others parents and who weren't part of any after school curriculums, unless you'd count after school detentions as such. Honestly, I hung with a group of kids whose parents (like my own) often couldn't afford to keep their kids in things like gymnastics or baseball and it wasn't always because they were bad or lazy parents either. As my number of peers grew in two differing communities so did my insight into how many other families had to live and conduct their homes. Sometimes, you would see good, honest and hard working people who never did drugs, didn't drink or smoke and still were struggling to keep food on the table and a roof over their families head.

Take my parents for example. Besides my dad's occasional beer or Margarita here and there, he was not an alcoholic and not a man known to waste or spend his money unwisely. I often heard of him and my step mom going away on nice vacations to places like Hawaii, Vegas, New Mexico, New Orleans and so on. With him and his wife both working they did well and didn't seem to struggle much financially, my mom on the other hand, back home in Bridgeview never drank or smoked and yet I remember her working 2 jobs and renting a bedroom so we could eat and keep the mortgage on our house paid.

I got to see a lot of things but one thing is for sure, rich or poor, I was associated with kids that a lot of parents wouldn't have wanted their own kids hanging out with. I remember Glenn Danzig, former singer of the punk rock band The Misfits releasing a solo album in 1988 with a song called Mother on it and me thinking to myself "Well, yeah, that pretty much says it all."

The first line of that song was "Mother, tell your children not to walk my way."

I was 12 years old trying to act 30 and in so many ways feeling as if I had already been to hell and back and having resolved somewhat deeply inside to the fact that my existence in this life was not going to end up with what I had been seeing on The Brady Bunch, I was a bit disillusioned after my mom and I stopped attending Church. I wasn't plugged into or associating with "Good Church Kids." I guess you could say that I went into my teenage years making friends with what some would call the "Bad Unchurched Kids."

Meanwhile, at my mom's house in Bridgeview during the school week, my friends and I would go to each other's houses (wherever parents weren't) and turn stereos up as loud as we could and bang our heads to metal bands like Slayer, Anthrax, Megadeth and Metallica. Our crazy youth being fueled by much Pepsi, nicotine and rage, we would play very loud music and start these violent mosh pits. I guess this was our way to feel big and at the same time shed off some of that pent up, negative, hurt and angry energy we had been accumulating from our own broken homes and young life experiences.

I can remember walking home from Jr. high in Justice IL. with friends of mine who would jump on the hoods of cars, punch mailboxes and do whatever they felt like to break all the rules. I guess in a way trying to impress one another. It was growing up with experiences like this that has persuaded me to the conclusion that kids raising kids without any sane adult supervision and guidance can end up becoming a very dangerous and destructive thing for youth in a community pretty fast.

A quick side note to parents, including myself, who is the proud Father of three great kids! We really need to be on guard for such things. Being aware of who our kids are hanging out with and keeping them close and intentionally making it an effort to be involved in their lives, especially with all the evil influences that are out there running rampant in this world. We as parents have to stay close and involved. I'm not saying we have to be all up in their grill, smothering them over every little thing but we do need to be very nearby and aware of what and who they are getting into. We have to be intentional about this and be ready to make adjustments in their young sails if we see them beginning to veer off course.

Growing up, many of us kids were from broken homes that had been ravished by poverty, drugs, alcohol, violence and divorce and we were being raised in environments where parents had to work a lot just to keep the minimums paid.

So here we were, unsupervised kids acting all buckwild in the streets with no parental guidance, becoming more and more like what I saw happening to my brother and his friends when I was 5, being taught how to light cigarettes off the stove. I used to laugh at those "I learned it from watching you" anti-drug commercials that were popular in the 1980's but in hindsight, I guess there was some truth to be found in them. Years later, having had my own brain fried on drugs, I must conclude, I was young and foolish for laughing at them. Many of my childhood friends had addicted parents. Many had messed up brothers and sisters. Many were wearing thrift store shoes and had the hand me downs in an 80's culture that was glorifying wealth and material excess. Many of my friends didn't see their families much and many of them were just kids emulating much of what they had seen being done and practiced when they did. We were kids living out what we had seen and what we had learned watching others we were looking up to. We were a lot like what Jesus said of the religious leaders of his own day and age, we were like *"The blind leading the blind."*

In a world where many are living and trying to figure this life out in the absence of a Good Father, there is nothing better than connecting people with the teachings of Jesus that reveal to us the heart and love of Our Heavenly Father. No matter what age, young or old, whether seven or seventy, there is no time like now to be aware of and connected over and over again to your Creator.

Let me get spiritual here for a moment.

We can take a look at Matthew 15:10-14.

Jesus replied,

"They are blind guides leading the blind, and if one blind person guides another, they will both fall into a ditch."
~ Matthew 15:13-14

Let me jump ahead in my life for a quick teachable moment, briefly before returning to my story here.

Later on in life, when I was 28 years old, my wife and I were expecting Joshua, my first born child and I still had myself a pretty bad cigarette habit. Now, by this time, with God's mercy, help and grace I had already shed some other nasty habits like heroin and cocaine, which I will get into in a little bit here but when it came to those cigarettes, I was still hanging onto Jane. Now, I know it sounds kind of weird but by the time I was 28 years old I had already been smoking some 16 years. At times I was even up to a pack and 1/2 a day. When I met my wife, and we were expecting our first child together, I was down to 1/2 a pack and for me, that in itself was nothing short of a miracle.

I was working hard in the corrugated box industry feeding large sheets of cardboard into what they called flexo machines 12 hours a day, 6 days a week and after the weeks pay was given to our rent, food, electric, insurance, phones, diapers, gas and so on... We were pretty much strapped and the price of those cigarettes just kept getting higher and higher. Plus, to top it all off, my wife didn't smoke at all and I was having to go outside on our apartment patio (come rain, hail or snow) to keep the smell of it from coming in the apartment near her and the baby. As addicted as I was, I really didn't want to be.

I had heard all the news about the health ramifications and I knew that I was trapped in something that I really didn't want to be in. The problem was that I was completely bound. Bound until I was graced by God to change the way I was thinking about it. It was at this time that I had heard a Christian song on the radio that really helped me alot. It was a song about a Father who wanted to be just like Jesus because he saw that his son wanted to be just like him. That song wrecked me at my core and I remember thinking to myself "I don't want to be doing anything in this life that I wouldn't want my son to be doing in his."

So that was it. After a few months of honest failed attempts and many nights sitting in a park telling God "This is going to be my last one", I with His help and continual confession of this weakness along with my admitted need for his help and grace in my life, I was finally able to find the strength I needed to break away from that nasty, old, unhealthy and expensive habit. That was God's Grace.

This is my health and prosperity gospel. Start by giving up all of your unhealthy and expensive habits. You will immediately become healthier and wealthier.

To anyone who knows the struggle though, I simply kept going to The Lord with it and telling him that I really needed his help with this and eventually we got it together. I can't tell you how many times I sat in his presence though with a cigarette in my hand smoking and telling him that I really needed his help with this. I even had this quiet place in a park that I would go to and I must have told God a couple dozen times that this was going to be my last cigarette, only to return the next evening or two days later with another one in my hand saying "Okay Lord, here we go again, now this is going to be my last."

Eventually though, not based on my own merit and effort alone but based more on his faithfulness, power and grace, it was as if even the desire to smoke was just one day taken away from me...

You see, His grace is always more than enough to overcome anything we are facing. I have found this to be true not only when we are facing hardships and persecution, like the stuff The Apostle Paul had written about in 2nd Corinthians 11 and 12 but as well in our own personal battles against unhealthy vices and addictions that can bring similar oppression and hardship on our lives.

Listen, no matter what we are facing or going through physically, emotionally or spiritually, God's Grace is all we truly need to find victory and freedom.

When looking specifically at 2nd Corinthians 12:9, God's Word to Paul in The Bible after he had pleaded 3 times for God to take away this *Thorn in His Flesh,* which I believe was as he had said it was, a messenger of Satan, sent to torment him, perhaps, God's Word to Paul that day wasn't meant to be taken as a resolve but rather as an imploring to open up and receive more of God's grace in exchange for that oppressive thing in his life. To me it was almost as if he was saying, "Be strengthened Paul, get up and keep going, my power and grace is more than enough and it is all you will need to overcome this and finish the work I have given you to do."

After Paul had pleaded 3 times with God to take this torment away…

"Each time he said, "My grace is all you need. My power works best in weakness."
~ 2nd Corinthians 12:9

My prayer right now, for all who are reading this, is that God's Power, Love and Grace would be poured out mightily on all things that have been contending with and tormenting any of our lives, be it poverty, addiction, fear, greed, lust, sickness, pain, persecution or vice.

Father God, I ask you to set all my readers free, and to empower us all with your power from heaven so that we all may collectively get up and continue to move forward into all you have ordained and called us to. Fill us with a fresh newness and awareness of your continued goodness and presence in our lives. ~ Amen

Chapter Eight

Boom

So now back to being a kid in Bridgeview with my mom and in Evergreen Park on the weekends with my dad. Let me just say, that things could get pretty nuts. My friends out in Evergreen were all into girls, drinking and blowing things up. We would sneak out at night while our parents were sleeping and spend all night walking around the neighborhood talking about things that we could explode. Half sticks of dynamite, M80's and match head bombs were a favorite pastime for us boys. I had this one particular friend Dennis who was obsessed with this kind of stuff. The bigger the boom the bigger his laugh and excitement!

He taught us all how we could make stalls with lit cigarettes and I remember going with him in the middle of the night once to duct tape explosives to the mailbox of someone he didn't like. Many of our weekend nights were spent out there at my dad's, roaming the streets reeking small havoc all over Evergreen Park. Everything from placing a steel pole across train tracks causing the stops to lower and stop traffic, to throwing tomatoes at cars from a local overpass, to tipping over a grease trap behind a popular local restaurant or launching water balloons with a three person slingshot into block parties.

If it was crazy, wrong and mischievous, we probably did it.

Anything a kid could come up with for a good laugh and thrill, we were down for it and thankfully by the grace of God, no one was hurt and we all came out of our adolescence with all of our extremities still intact.

Me and Mike (the golfer) used to gather golf balls from the outskirts of the local golf course in Evergreen and resell them, four for a dollar back to the golfers in their golf carts. At 14 years old we didn't have jobs, so this became a means to buy snacks and cigarettes from a vending machine at the local bowling alley. I can remember being with my friends walking down a busy street like 95th and California in Evergreen smoking, swearing at each other, acting all tough and bad and then freaking out and hiding like scared little kids anytime one of us thought we may have seen a car that looked like one of our parents.

Smoking cigarettes, hopping trains, cussing, sneaking out all night, trying to impress girls and blowing up mailboxes. My friends in my adolescent years.

By the time I was 14 and in 8th grade we had also developed an infatuation with Rock Concerts as well. Some years earlier when I was 9 years old I got to see Ozzy Osbourne and Metallica with my cousin Terry. I was in the 7th row standing on my chair, and Ozzy pointed at me saying "We have some little rockers out here tonight." I also peed next to Cliff Burton, the bass player from Metallica in the bathroom. I thought to myself ,"This is so awesome." As an adolescent, my friends and I would ride trains and buses to downtown Chicago and see tons of metal bands play. A lot of bands who became very popular but who were not mainstream popular yet. I remember getting to see Pantera in a small club called The Avalon under the L tracks on their Cowboys from Hell tour and another time being in a tattoo parlor while Dimebag Darrell (their guitar player) got a new tattoo. I got my first tattoo at 15. We saw White Zombie in a small club, when all they had as a stage show were a strand of Christmas lights around the bass drum. I saw Clash of the Titans, Nine Inch Nails, the first Lollapalooza, Rush, Metal Fest… Honestly, the list of bands we saw and the stories I could tell about being kids at rock concerts can go on and on. I was at the filming of three music videos that got regular airtime on M.T.V's Headbangers Ball and was just completely submerged in that whole metal head scene. I had a black jacket that my mom had hand sown metal band patches all over for me. All before I was 16 years old, I had been to enough concerts to last a young person a lifetime.

I also always had one girl who I was always madly and secretly in love with but was always way too shy to actually say anything to her about it. This became quite the norm for me growing up. While all my friends were getting lucky and hooking up with different girls, I was always the guy who just ended up friends with the girl that I secretly had a crush on.

I just truly had no moves. I have always been the guy with no moves. I was always very shy and selective. In part, I believe being raised by a single mom coupled with the absence of my dad in my daily life, left a deep longing in me to know what it meant to "Be a Man" and in this longing to find that answer, it led me into a love for stories about chivalry and knighthood.

For the record. I have never been a player. I am not a player and I don't want to have anything to do with the game. I have always been awe struck with the idea of real, romantic and committed love, followed by marriage and a healthy family. I always have been and I always will be a one woman kind of guy.

Fighting as well became a staple of my youth.

My dad says he remembers a season in which it seemed like every time I came to see him he was getting word from my mom that I had got suspended again from school for another fight. Now it's true that I was getting into fights quite a bit but it wasn't because I was mean. It was because I was weird. If someone just looked at me the wrong way and slurred something under their breath at me, like loser or fag because I had long hair, I was ready to throw down right there in the school hallway. I had this thing as well for all of the bullies in school. If there was a bully at school, I had to have my shot at him. I believe in hindsight, this may have come from me being bullied by my mom and not being able to retaliate as a kid. My mom says that she was hard on me as a kid in an attempt to toughen me up for this mean world. She says that knowing I didn't have a Father around, she was trying to play both roles as a single parent. Whatever her reasoning or justification, let me just say, that being mocked or slapped can make you feel pretty defenseless, so as I grew older, whenever I saw something similar happening to someone else, this strong almost uncontrollable compulsion would rise up inside of me and I would have to step up and defend the oppressed one involved. I knew too well what it was like to just have to take abuse from someone and not be able to do anything about it. So in school, when I saw similar injustices going on, I always took the opportunity to do something about it.

On every account, I was the kid that would either be defending myself from bullies or be the one going after the kid who was bullying someone else. I had no tolerance for this kind of stuff and I would snap off in a heartbeat over it. I guess in many ways, you can say that my mom helped raise me to be a fighter. At one point, in Junior high, I remember there was this kid who kept making fun of me at school, so my mom, instead of telling me to go and tell the teacher, went out, bought me boxing gloves from The Salvation Army and taught me how to throw my first punch. The next day at school after this bully opened his mouth at me, I stood up and hit him in his face and I got what they called a 2 day in school suspension. My mom on the other hand took me out for dinner that evening, happy that I had stood up for myself. From that point on, with mom's approval, I was never afraid to go toe to toe with even the meanest of them. Not sure if this was brave or smart. It just was.

All of the above and more had become my life leading up to this point but please understand that despite the youthful lusts, passions, emotions and craziness we all have endured growing up... I did have my limits.

Playing girls and doing drugs were boundaries I had always refused to cross. I was very strong in my convictions about these two things and very vocal with my friends about this. So, besides me and my friends little drinking here and there, a couple of my friends' obsession with dirty magazines, our bad language and unhealthy smoking habits, I was against divulging in much more.

I mean even at 14 years old, I had my boundaries.

As a kid, I had witnessed what drugs had done to my older brother's life and I can remember going to see and visit him with my dad and stepmom in The Palos Hospital Rehabilitation Center and hearing him talk about his hope to stay clean and clear of his addictions.

I was 11 when my brother Mark had come out of the hospital and over the next few years he started to resurface back into me and my mom's life on a pretty regular basis. He was clean now and on so many levels becoming a role model that I could honestly look up to. He was 19 and sober, probably for the 1st time since he'd been 11 himself and he had recently developed what he kept telling everyone around him was a personal relationship with Jesus Christ.

I believed it was because of that note I put in the pastor's hand.

Mark and his new Christian girlfriend Shauna were getting serious and going to a local baptist church together and I was so excited to hear that he had got off those stupid drugs. I was even happier to see him and my mom getting along again. Him and my dad had been out of our lives for sometime now and my mom was beyond happy to have her son back.

I knew without a doubt that it was him getting clean and finding Jesus that was helping at least part of our family to reconcile. Even at 11 years old, I had enough insight by this time to know who all the good things in life were actually coming from.

"Every good and perfect gift is from above, coming down from the Father of the heavenly lights, who does not change like shifting shadows." ~ James 1:27

My mom was doing a lot better as well. She had found some happiness dating a childhood friend of hers who had recently gone through a nasty divorce himself. He would come over on weekends and bring his son "Little Larry" who was a few years younger than me. My mom's boyfriend was "Big Larry" and he took me fishing a couple times and would always be over on Friday nights to eat popcorn and watch rented movies with me and my mom. He was a really nice guy who was always light hearted and smiled a lot.

I was young and had already been through some pretty low lows and rebounded on some pretty high highs in life and whether I was with my friends in Bridgeview or in Evergreen, I was still breathing, my brother was back around and him and his soon to be wife were becoming shining examples to me, as they were seeking to make Jesus Christ the center of everything in their lives. It seemed to me clearly at this point, that everything good in life was coming as a result of people being with this Jesus and that everything bad and broken was a direct result of people not knowing him or continuing to go on without him.

The sum of all these experiences, all became such a tipping point for me as a child. My mom was doing a million miles better than she was during her nervous breakdown and now she was working a new job with better pay as a medical records clerk at Loyola Medical Center in Oak Forest. All of this and my brother's new found decision to make Jesus Lord and Savior of his life…

Well, this had me basking and ecstatic in the providential, delivering graces and goodness of God.

Regardless of my "Unchurched" and often misguided friends, it all was like a long awaited prayer being answered for me to see all of these good things coming to pass at home, and to see so quickly what seemed like years of depression, confusion, heartache and pain being transformed into healing, hope, purpose and joy. It was like all of a sudden Jesus had showed up and He was making all things new.

One steadfast constant in my life, that I have come to rely on is that with Jesus, things just always seem to keep getting better and better for us but apart from him things can begin to wither and perish and go bad really fast.

In Christ's own words he said;

"Remain in me, and I will remain in you. For a branch cannot produce fruit if it is severed from the vine, and you cannot be fruitful unless you remain in me." ~ John 15:4

And he also said;

"I have told you these things, so that in me you may have peace. In this world you will have trouble. But take heart! I have overcome the world." ~ John 16:33

Chapter Nine

Come Sail Away

"The Sky so thoughtfully molded. Like a painting that could not be ruined. A peace surpassing all things. As my eyes still seek the sun. Without rest. I feel so awake as the morning takes it's course. I see no pain and I see no one destined to be hurt."

Before I go on and tell you anything further about how beautiful it was to see my brother back and filled with this fresh zeal for Jesus, I want to backstep just a little bit here to explain how important literature had become to me in my younger years. The words above are from a poem I had written when I was 12 years old. I was sitting on the swing in front of my mom's house watching the sun rise. I had been up all night thinking again (as I was accustomed to) and as the sun came up, I sat on the front porch with a notebook and pen in my hand, writing down these words. It's some 31 years later and I can still remember this poem coming to my heart and mind like it was yesterday. It was one of those times in which I felt like something that had already been written in heaven somewhere was being given to me here in that moment on earth that day.

As a lifelong writer of songs, poetry and anything else I can write about, I have written a lot of stuff over the years. Notebooks and notebooks as a kid that would fill up with my words, thoughts and ink. My mom actually has a suitcase filled with my writings. At times, I have seen this infatuation as a gift that was given to me by God to help me process and make sense of all the confusing ordeals of my young life and at lesser times of reflection, I could just chalk it all up to a child's overactive mind and imagination. The gift sometimes seemed more like a relentless, restlessness of intellect that just liked to keep me up all night like a curse. Even unto this day, at bedtime sometimes my wife will have to tell me in a way like no one else can, "It's time to turn the thinkers off." She knows me and balances me well.

You see, I have always been an introvert, a ponderer, a reader and a thinker. As a kid, I loved the deep thinking that The Bible would provoke and I can honestly say that The Holy Bible is the book that I learned how to read and process things with. I was internalizing The Psalms and Proverbs at 7 and 8 years old and of all the books I have ever read, The Bible has been and still is my favorite... It truly is more... So much more than just a book.

It is the God Inspired writings and teachings of many prophets, poets, kings, apostles and priests. It is also The

Book that contains The Red Letter teachings of Jesus Christ himself. God in the flesh, come to show humanity The Father's Love and Ways.

By the time I was a freshman in highschool, I was 6 years ahead of my peers and was taking a sophomore college level English class. I had advanced easily in literature while letting everything else fall by the wayside. In math class, when I should have been doing algebra, I was off in my own little world writing about love and rhyming my words in ways to make points. I loved Emerson and Thoreau and everything out of the transcendentalist era. I was in love with all concepts of love and anything that had to do with chivalry, nobility, defending the weak and restoring justice to the land. If it had anything to do with good overcoming evil or mercy having it's triumph over judgement, I was totally interested and fully engaged. The dark side though, to this obsession to excel in the literature arts, was not only the deep neuropath ways I assuredly had dug into my brains surface but the way I had also found them as a place to hide and escape into. Today, as an objective adult, I can tell you confidently that as a child I had used this "Land of Literature" in many ways as a means of escaping the harsh realities of my often own hard life. I was then as a child and still even now as an adult a hopeless dreamer. You see, outside the imaginary land of reading and envisioning utopia like existences here on Earth, there was this reality of all the family problems and real life issues that were always brewing and boiling over at home. In the years prior to my brother's miraculous deliverance from drugs and alcohol, I had really delved myself pretty deep into varying worlds of album art, lyrics, books and poems and before my brother became a Christian and before any reconciliation had begun in our lives as brothers again, I was already getting deeper and deeper into reading and listening to music. During those years that my Father had left and I had to experience my Mother's fight to keep her sanity... In all of those turbulent years, I had found great comfort and peace, often alone in solitude with literature and music.

So here I was, a child who on one hand could delve deep into inspiring and thought provoking writings that birthed great hope to my young heart while on the other hand could be drawn into all the hurt, sadness and angst that other works of great literacy or music might provoke. All the tales of struggle and great hardship endured and overcome by so many noble characters in history were stories that (even as a child) I was already able to grasp and greatly identify with. So depending on the musings of my day, I could either become extremely optimistic or deeply depressed and it was all pretty contingent on what kind of art, literature or music I was entertaining.

For example; My attitude was a lot more chipper on the days I was into The Apostle Paul's book of Philippians than let's say the days I was entrenched in Edgar Allen Poe. "All You Need is Love" by Paul Mccartney of The Beatles always seemed to pick me up a bit more than let's say "The Downward Spiral" by Trent Reznor. Now please don't get me wrong. I'm not trying to say anything derogatory about either Poe or Trent. Trent Reznor of Nine Inch Nails honesty and transparency about who he is and all the darkness he has embodied and wrestled with in my opinion is something to be observed and learned from but not necessarily a path I would encourage anyone to follow and likewise for Edgar Allan Poe to entertain us with such dark recesses of thought and imagination, a lot like Stephen King or M. Night Shyamalan is a fearless journey of uninhibited thought and dark expression that not just anyone could possess and articulate.

So whether someone's art was something that brought me up or down, left me excited or scared, comforted or confused...

My point here is that there is so much beautiful, broken, good and bad, messy vastness of expressions spreading across wide spectrums of diversity in us as humans and I have found that there will always be art, music and literature created that can and will affirm all of God or the devil's negative and positive impressions upon us. In other words, there is pretty much art out there to encourage any thought or emotion we may be having at any time. Be that good or bad, from Heaven or Hell.

So for me, the pursuit of art, literature and music was a lot like how the internet is being used by many of us today. Whether something is right, wrong or indifferent, you can always find a search engine that will pull up some related article, blog, youtube clip, song or post that will come into agreement with how you are feeling about practically any given situation. Before the internet, I found the same affirmations in words, movies, music and art.

For example; When I was young and coming of age, desiring the love of some young fair lady, songs like Peter Gabriel's "In Your Eyes" and Led Zeppelin's "Thank You" spoke volumes to my young lovestruck heart, while The Velvet Underground's Heroin and Tupac Shakur's album "Me Against The World" became like anthems that I sang on my quick, misled descent into Chicago's drug culture.

Before I go any deeper into my broken love story here, let me take the liberty here to get spiritual again for a moment.

Bill Johnson (A minister and author whom I enjoy) points out in his book "The Supernatural Power of a Renewed Mind" that God was able to send a storm to get Jonah (of The Bible) back in line with His will for his life, while the devil on the other hand was able to stir one up against the disciples on a boat to try and get them out of it. This is a profound point. Bill Johnson then teaches (better than I'm paraphrasing) how important it is to know whose storm is coming when those winds start blowing.

This revelation alone caused me to begin reviewing my life and brought me to a much needed clarity on something I want to share with you all right now. Today, I can see just how many storms of the enemy and hardships I have had to endure in this life simply because I had no real spiritual discernment of whose whirlwinds they were.

Let me explain. As The Apostle Paul had once written.

"When I was a child, I talked like a child, I thought like a child, I reasoned like a child. When I became a man, I put the ways of childhood behind" ~ *1st Corinthians 13:11*

You see, whether our minds have been taking on an onslaught of arrows (negative words and thoughts) from the enemy or the brushing embraces of angelic messages and encounters (insight and revelation) from God, my prayer for you and me is that the underlying message in the remainder of this book would be like a strong rushing wind of God's Love, Presence, Grace and Revelation flowing powerfully from His Heavenly Throne to us all.

Father God, I pray that my testimony of Jesus and how my faith in your son has not only redeemed me from the muck and mire that the accuser was trying to bury me in but as well has reconciled me to you, Our Father, creator, our source and sustainer, our healer and deliverer and that you, above all, will bring all of my readers' minds, souls and hearts into a deeper revelation of you and your son's love, mercy and forgiveness for us all.

Today, I know more than ever how important it is for me to be aware of and be on guard of whose inspiration, art and impartations I am entertaining, allowing and receiving. The importance of being on guard of whose will and inspirations are trying to get into my mind, soul, body and heart. You see, Jesus was very clear on this;

"The thief comes only to steal and kill and destroy; I have come that they may have life, and have it to the full. ~ John 10:10

   As I have aged and been made more clearly aware of these two opposing wills in my life (God's and the devil's) I have to remain fixed and stand my ground as the guardian at my own gate, choosing wisely whose inspirations and impartations I am going to allow in. Unlike when I was a child, letting anyone in to say and do whatever they wanted, I am now a grown man seeking The Father's Heart, His Will and His Plan for my life. Today, I am seeking the art, music, literature and inspirations that will inspire that end goal of my life.

Christ's Plans and Purposes for me.

   I have to continually be on guard as to whose thoughts, reports, teachings, inspirations and philosophies, I am going to agree with and allow into the castle of my own vast mind, soul and heart. As many differing thoughts and influences will continue to come and go, as a man, I am ever ready to shod my feet today, take up My Shield of Faith and say to all who come "Halt" and "Who goes there?"

It's crucial for me to test these spirits (thoughts and inspirations) and to know whose wind is blowing when I encounter any kind of storm in my life. I need to be on guard of whose messengers and messages are being sent my way. I have to ask myself "Are these winds angelic or demonic? Are they on course with God's Will for my life or not?"

More pointedly as a Minister of Jesus Christ, I would like to say that all songs, literature, movies, art, philosophies and search engines that seek to get us in agreement with anything less than what God Our Father has willed and planned for us are to be treated the same as above. Ask yourself if what you are entertaining on a regular basis is contributing to or taking you away from your true identity in Christ?

Today, I have found that by praying in The Spirit and renewing our minds to The Truths found in a correct understanding and teaching of The Bible, we can all come to know more clearly God's revealed heart and will for us all.

I have personally found, after at least 37 years of searching, that knowing God, ultimately means to know and experience his deep love and forgiveness for us all.

My prayer is that from this word fourth, regardless of your present age, that we can all be more aware of and on greater guard together of all the enemy's lies and distracting storms he may be trying to send through various forms of art, media, music, film and literature in an attempt to get us off of God's directives and good course for our life.

Let us Trust God with all our heart, mind and soul and let's not lean on our own understanding of things but rather learn to rest, lean on and incline unto Him as our Father, as children would rest and incline into their own Father's arms, learning to listen and get our direction from Him and sensing where God's heart winds are going and willing to let Him adjust our own sails, if need be, so we can all be more in line with where Heaven's Atmosphere is moving here on Earth.

Chapter Ten

My Generation

The impact music and lyrics had on us as kids was unparalleled. Those loud expressions of emotion gave us youth who didn't really like much of what we were seeing in this world an anthem to sing to and a rebellion to die for. The anti-establishment undertones to be found in much of our generation's music was very compelling and fueling to say the least. We were part of an underground subculture whose temperature was always set to fed up. We had been swallowed up and enveloped into a world of rock, rap, metal, punk and goth that my friends and I were all seeking to emulate and imitate in all manners of dress, attitude, speech and deed.

Going into my high school years, this subculture that was unfolding all around me was progressively getting darker and darker, while the light my brother Mark and his wife Shauna were shining and talking about was growing brighter and brighter. Mark and Shauna were becoming a real integral part of my life at this time and they were always at my mom's house in Bridgeview. My mom would cook these huge Sunday afternoon meals that were enough to feed a small army and would always send my brother and his wife home with enough food to darn near carry them through till our next Sunday gathering.

My brother was totally in love with Jesus and he was always telling me and my friends about how much God loved us. By the time, he had resurfaced from his addictions as A New Creature in Christ, I had been banging on those drums after school and writing lyrics for some time now. So when he came to me with the idea of wanting to start a "Christian Rock Band" I was elated! I mean wow! How about that! My drug addicted brother who I had prayed for and placed letters into the hands of Pastor Phillip Epperson about, was now clean and sober and wanting me to make rock music for Jesus with him. So we did the next logical thing and started a Christian Rock band. My brother on guitar and me on drums. Here I was, a teenager now, with long hair, wearing Ozzy Osbourne T-shirts, getting ready to rock it out for Jesus in a band with my brother. I had never been happier! Our first band name was "Admonish" which we had taken from Colossians 3:16;

*"Let the message of Christ dwell among you richly as you teach and **admonish** one another with all wisdom through psalms, hymns, and songs from the Spirit, singing to God with gratitude in your hearts."*

He wrote all the music and I wrote all the lyrics. I was in my first year of high school playing drums and writing lyrics in my brother's "Christian Rock Band" and we had a mission to "Rock The World With The Word."

This was our first song and I can still remember writing the first line.

"All these strange days of war and decay corrupting the minds of our future."

My brother and I were determined to shine a light in this world that we both knew could get pretty dark at times. For about a year, we practiced and wrote songs every week and tried to bring a couple others on board with us but they just didn't get what we were doing. You see, there was a lot of Christian Rock music around at the time like Petra and Stryper but we were writing music that sounded more like the secular music of Megadeth or Pantera.

As a matter of fact, in 1990 by the time I was 14, not many in the christian communities understood us at all. We were a bit rough around the edges. We smoked cigarettes, wore leather jackets and had hair longer than The Beatles. Plus, we were writing music that was way heavier than your average contemporary Christian Rock. I mean, this wasn't Michael W. Smith stuff. By the way, I love Mr. Smith. He's a Powerful Man of God, it's just that we were more like Slayer baptized in The Holy Spirit kind of stuff…

At one point, we had even visited a huge local megachurch not too far from our hometown in Bridgeview. The first one I had ever seen and my brother asked the Youth Pastor if it would be alright for us to post a flier on their bulletin board looking for a singer and bass player to join our Christian Band. My brother was told that we couldn't do that unless we were committed active members of their church. Neither of us really got or understood this, so what ended up happening was that one of my buddies from school Ernie started to learn how to play bass and we ended up with another rare Christian Metalhead named Sparky. A kid who responded to an ad we had thrown in a completely secular local newspaper and this was how "Christian" our Speed Metal Christian Rock band was born. We changed our name from "Admonish" to "Christian" and practiced at my mom's house in her front room twice a week, until we had a strong enough set and fan base to start playing live shows on the weekends.

We also started having these awesome bible studies. Remember all those "Unchurched kids" I was talking about earlier, all my outcast friends who were raging against the machine? They all ended up sitting in my mom's front room with open hearts and open bibles every Tuesday and Thursday night right before we would start our very loud band practices.

I remember one evening counting 60 kids coming in and out. All of these goth, rock, skater, metalhead and hippy kids. You name it. They all gravitated to our practices like mosquitoes to a bug light and they were all getting zapped. Zapped by God.

Many of them smoked and cussed and some even had tattoos.

We really weren't the good "Youth Group" kind of kids one might expect to find at a bible study 2 times a week. Nonetheless, we were listening to my brother Mark and learning The Bible and hearing The True Gospel of Christ's Forgiveness, The Holy Spirit and total acceptance and love of one another.

My brother's wife Shauna who was and still is like a big sister to me, always was our biggest fan and cheerleader and she always brought a real positive vibe to all we were doing for Jesus. We were kids getting right with God, staying out of trouble and receiving newness of life from the red letter teachings of Christ. My brother never really did get into much of The Old Testament stuff. He pretty much kept us all well fed with The New Testament stuff, the parables of The Kingdom and the teachings of Jesus himself. All that good Kingdom, Joy, Peace and Love kind of stuff. The Good News!

By the time I was 15 years old, I was playing 21 and over nightclubs in a band that would proclaim Jesus very boldly and loudly via the medium of some very heavy and fast metal music. Our frontman Sparky deemed us the inventors of what he had coined "Adrenaline Metal."

My brother Mark, at every show, would always take time at the mic to tell these clubs, venues, gymnasiums and bars all about God's love for them, His Son Jesus and forgiveness. We never played a show that my brother didn't give his testimony of deliverance and lead us all through some sort of invitation or Sinner's Prayer.

Let me say that as controversial as "A Sinner's Prayer" is to some these days, that prayer meant a lot to many of us and we felt very honored to be able to share that invitation from our hearts in places many Christians would never go.

We were young and really didn't have much of a theology. All we knew was that if people would repent, change their thinking and ask Jesus into their lives, believe that he had died for their sins and was resurrected again for their life and begin confessing him as their Lord and Savior that they'd be saved and that The Holy Spirit would take care of them as they continued in their relationship with Him and in His word. That was our young, simple, childlike faith and theology.

It was all pretty phenomenal. There wasn't anywhere we wouldn't go and proclaim The Gospel of Jesus. I mean we opened for bands like "Nuclear Assault" at The Aragon Ballroom in Chicago. We would travel to Southern Illinois, Indiana, Michigan and St. Louis. We played in nightclubs that G.G. Allen, a notorious shock rocker who would cut himself and every halloween threaten to commit suicide on stage had been immortalized in. This particular club for example in Muskegon Michigan was graffitied with spray paint from top to bottom and after we were done playing our set there and proclaiming The Good News of Jesus Christ, we were given a can of spray paint and the honor to add our band name "Christian" to their dive club wall.

We were greatly honored.

God gifted us to stand our ground in a pretty rough scene of music and by the time my brother Mark would speak, these kids in mosh pits or these older alcoholics and addicts in bars would all actually stop, draw near and listen. It was a beautiful thing to see The Gospel being proclaimed to people who needed to hear it.

I recall being 15 years old in this club called The Thirsty Whale, a place in Chicago that was known for many popular acts and on a night when we were headlining, I remember standing in the bathroom with our band singing Maranatha praise songs like "Lord, I lift your name on high" and "I love You Lord", right before going out onstage to play speed metal songs as tight and fast as Megadeth with hooks as muddy and heavy as Sabbath.

In my own mind, I was a 15 year old rock star writing lyrics that I hoped could change the world. Mostly lyrics that reflected and expressed my own brokenness and hope of healing and restoration. Read this line I wrote and that our front man "Sparky" must have sang live hundreds of times.

"Our day has come, Thy will is done, evil is casted away we are yours for eternity, you came for me, you came for me, second coming, second coming, No more demons from your past, bad memories are done with, the time has come to descend from the sky, you came for me, you come for me, second coming." ~ The Battle Rages On

Eventually my brother Mark and his wife Shauna had two children back to back, making me the proud uncle of Micah and Corey, two awesome and talented, smart and gifted young men in their own right and as my brothers family was growing, so was his new responsibilities as a Husband, a Provider and a Father.

This also meant more work, bigger bills and less time to focus on the band and ministry. Inevitably, all those demands between family, work and ministry eventually all began to wear thin on my brother and as well on his marriage and home life.

As he tried to hold down a job by day as a machinist and tried to keep the momentum of the band, bible studies and weekend gigs booked by night, it was all just really becoming and understandably so, too much for a young married couple with two babies at home to keep up with. He was only 23 years old.

It was also around this same time that our bass player got his girlfriend pregnant and tensions were beginning to rise between me and Sparky about our musical direction. I was getting more and more into newer bands like "Rage Against The Machine" and "Korn" while Sparky started doing gigs on the side with other local musicians that were much more musically technical and not Christ oriented.

Not even a year later, Sparky our frontman left the band and we would be looking for a new singer to front our now battered mission.

Despite the growing opposition, new obstacles and setbacks my brother and I were facing, we were determined to press on and try to weather these storms. We regrouped with a great bass player and childhood friend of mine named Jack, now with The Chicago based band The Citizens and we threw my punk rocker buddy Don up on the stage with his Ian Mackaye of Fugazi and Minor Threat vocal style. With Jack on bass and our new front man Don heading out these shows, we recorded to date what I believe was our best demo tape ever.

An 8 song demo tape released in 1993 called "Bent".

In hindsight, I believe there was a powerful anointing on where God was willing all of this to go for us. Me and my brothers musical chemistry over the years had really grown. He could make time signature changes in his playing that I could follow like some sort of musical telekinesis. We were just beginning to stumble upon some of his most powerful and inspiring guitar riffs ever. His playing was taking us all to a whole new level of glory and we were destined to "Rock This World With The Word" and then that's when it all happened.

Another storm...

Personally, I don't believe it was the kind of storm that was intended to knock us off track as much as it was the kind that is sent to try and knock you out of God's Will for good.

I must admit that I was a little shocked by the announcement that my brother was going to be leaving the band. Actually, devastated, would probably be more fitting. I mean, I was like a kid with a full paid scholarship. I thought that all I had to do was keep playing those drums and writing lyrics. I didn't have a plan B in my life. I was 17 years old. I was in the band of my dreams and had started dating a girl a year earlier who I was convinced I would marry. I had even saved up enough to buy her an engagement ring. Our band was getting better and better. Our live shows were full of so much energy and an atmosphere was being created in these places that made it seem as if anything was going to be possible and then that dooming announcement came. My brother said that his wife and kids needed him to be at home more.

Years later and as a Father of 3, I can totally understand this today. I understand and can say that I respect the fact that he chose to put his family first. It's a principle I myself learned from him and continue to live out in my own life and ministry. The problem I have is with what I saw go down after he made his decision to quit.

My brother walked away and that was it. It all had come to a quick, crashing end. I mean, he was the movement in so many ways and when the leader walked away so did the movement. We were all following his heart and dream, we could feel his faith and sincerity and really valued his teaching and what we were all learning in The Bible. The insights that came from the overflow of his own heart seeking and going after God but now without his passion, leading, his guitar riffs and anyone there to book our gigs and drive us to our shows, it was all abruptly over.

He was the man with the plan. I was following him. I had his back with my 10 Piece Tama Imperialstar drum kit for years… and now I was off course, directionless and a bit lost at sea.

I was 17 years old now and all of a sudden with a lot more extra time on my hands. So I ended up getting a job at a local pizza joint and continued onward as best as I could in high school. It went like this. I would get on a bus for school at 7:00, get out of school at 2:30, get on another bus, go eat lunch at the same place every day and then start work at 3:30. I wouldn't get home from work until 11:00. I worked six days a week and went to school five. I did this for about a year straight and must admit that as I focused more on work and getting that paycheck, my grades in high school really began to slip again.

My mom, God Bless her had got a hold of 800 dollars somehow and bought me my first car. A Blue Dodge Aries that she had surprised me with on my 17th birthday. She had Mark, the guy who gave me my first drum set, drive it up to me and park it in the parking lot of my job with a big red bow on it. Next to those drums, this was the second best gift I'd ever been given.

At this time in life, I was really in love with my fiance. She was my first real girlfriend and in trying to be a good Christian, I had bought her an engagement ring and had already asked her to marry me. I was young and in love and figured this was better to do than to continue "burning with passion" for her. We'd been going together since we were 15 and had seen each other practically every day for 2 years. She never missed a band practice and all my friends were her friends. For years we were inseparable but now with my new school and work schedule and no more band practices to meet up in, we were lucky if we got to see each other in quick passing in between classes. Our time together as a couple went from always together to practically never together.

For a season, my whole life seemed to be at work and school.

No more band. No more vision. No more hope of touring the world as Christian Rock Stars. Just school, work and that kind of depression that slowly slips in over one's life after they realize that all their dreams have been shattered. It was like Mr. Reality showed up one day, slapped me in my grandiose face and then kicked me in the backside saying "Hey, there is no time in this life for silly little pipe dreams, grow up now and go get a real job."

Today, as a husband, a father, a minister and a small business owner, I can not say enough about good "Time Management" and all the "Healthy Habits" of successful people I have studied and learned from. It is true that in order to rule over much and have highly productive lives we have to prioritize our time wisely and remain faithful to many mundane tasks that in the overall picture cause for a more well balanced, productive and effectual life. If perhaps there was as much access to these kinds of structural teachings available to my brother and I back in the 90's, maybe he could have held onto that musical ministry while not having to forsake his first God given priority which rightfully so, was his family. As I dove from the ministry myself into long hours at school and work, I guess my brother began falling slowly back into some of his old unhealthy habits again.

  Now, I already knew that in our ministry days he was always having to stand strong at his day job as a machinist amongst co-workers who liked to party and drink a lot. I remember one guy from his job who used to laugh about being so drunk that he went home and urinated in his wife's underwear drawer. Not the best atmosphere, to say the least, for my brother who had alcohol and substance abuse problems in his past. In order to stay sober, in the years we were in ministry together, he used to write bible verses on his red tool box with a black marker and he would always keep Jesus on his sleeve with everyone anywhere he would go. After the band broke up and our Bible Studies ceased and there was virtually no fellowship or accountability for any of us anymore... It wasn't long before he was isolating, drinking hard and smoking pot again. On the enemy's part, I believe it was all a really well crafted wile of...

"Smite the shepherd, and the sheep of the flock shall be scattered"
~ Matthew 26:31

On our part as lost, wandering, goth, skater, metalhead, punk rock youth with no one to lead us anymore it became...

"Where there is no vision, the people are unrestrained"
~ Proverbs 29:18

Chapter Eleven

Digging In The Dirt

Let me take the next few chapters of this book to till the soil a bit and get spiritual once again before I go into the hardest part of my story. Before I go into my heroin years, I need to do this...

First off, let me say that I do not believe in any way that God's unstoppable love for us is ever contingent on any of our own strivings and personal attempts at what I like to call Personal Holiness. Nor do I believe that Righteousness is something that is obtained by adhering to some man made or religious organization's list of do's and don'ts.

The healthiest theology I can find on this matter, is the study of Christ's life himself and how his love was granted and poured out lavishly on all who would simply believe and receive him right where they were, no matter who they were.

God's love is a gift that is given, not hard earned.

Lessons can be hard learned but God's love for us all is a given.

Let me explain this a little clearer.

Depending on what religious organization you may belong to, you might have found that at the core of many religious organizations there seems to be a list of rules and regulations that can drastically differ from each other.

For example;

~ Some Pentecostals may forbid any and all consumption of alcohol by the members of their congregation, while Lutheran and Catholic Priests can be found serving the real deal holyfield during their communions on Sunday.

~ Some Ministers may insist on a full immersion water baptism as an adult while others in Christendom may be alright with the simple dedication or communion they had received as a child.

~ Some Churches may like to scream, clap and shout really loud and get their praise on, while other places may insist that our God is not hard of hearing and believe that all of that is unhelpful and unneeded.

~ Some may want to turn it up and get all undignified like King David dancing and twirling around in dance while others might prefer to be more modest, reverent, reserved and still in his holy presence like one might be when listening to classical music or the singing of monks.

~ Some may say we should dress up in our Sundays best when going to The House of The Lord, while others will tell you to come in your jeans, work clothes and flannel just as you are.

The list can go on and on and honestly, what I believe most of us end up doing is just finding a group of believers that we can share some commonalities with. We ultimately go where we feel the most accepted, loved and comfortable. As they say, birds of the same feather flock together… Right?

So if you are a "Be still in His presence" kind of believer you may feel a bit challenged in let's say an all black, tongue talking, full gospel, hand clapping, floor stomping, storefront street ministry found on the Southside of Chicago. On the other hand, if you are a go getting, all out Holy Spirit filled, gift operating, devil stomping, empowered Child of The Most High God who likes to scream and shout, I would imagine you might feel a little quenched and maybe even a bit bored sitting in a Catholic Mass week after week.

All the above, I say not to stir up anymore dissension between us as Christians than our differing religious practices and cultures already have but rather I point such things out in the hope to promote greater diversity, understanding and unity within our collective worship that is all still within The Body of Christ.

As all members of One Body communing within the same Family of God, I believe it is important for us all to embrace one another's cultural and religious differences, all while working to maintain our faithfulness and commitment to love and serve one another.

"My command is this: Love each other as I have loved you."~ John 15:12

I personally know too well what it's like to feel like a fish in the wrong pond or a bird chirping in the wrong tree but I also know that God has truly created all the fish and all the ponds and all of the birds and all of the trees. God has created the sky, the earth, the sea and everything in between. Whether you are a black fish, gold fish, white fish, blue fish, green fish, yellow fish, red fish, brown fish, cold water, warm water, tropical fish, a pigeon, parakeet, eagle, crow, sparrow and so on... Jesus loves us all as much and even more and Our Father and Creator in

Heaven has fearfully and wonderfully knitted each and everyone of us together in our mother's womb.

"I praise you because I am fearfully and wonderfully made; your works are wonderful, I know that full well. My frame was not hidden from you when I was made in the secret place, when I was woven together in the depths of the earth. Your eyes saw my unformed body; all the days ordained for me were written in your book before one of them came to be." ~ *Psalms 139:14-16*

God knitted each one of us together with a strand of DNA that can literally be unravelled to the moon and back and as God's creation we were created for his pleasure and purposes... not for his punishing wrath and I personally don't believe we as humans have even begun to scratch the surface of our God given inherent potential.

I mean, we are talking about Our Father and Creator God, the one who can still the ocean, raise the sun and whose kid could walk on water. Oh, how unsearchable are the depths of knowledge and wisdom and power there is still to be found in this great mystery of Christ.

Christ in us, Our Hope of Glory...

"And this is the secret: Christ lives in you. This gives you assurance of sharing his glory." ~ Colossians 1:27

As Christ's Disciples we are called by God to become "Fishers of men." Knowing this, I have always been amazed at how fishermen using different colored lines and bait can catch different kinds of fish.

So be it with all of our own diversity in culture, music and worship gatherings that span so vastly across all of the land and sea.

"For as the waters fill the sea, the earth will be filled with an awareness of the glory of the LORD." ~ Habakkuk 2:14

Now, I do not believe for one minute that God Loved my brother Mark any more or any less when he was sober than when he was drinking and when I say drinking, I'm not talking about a glass of wine after dinner or a couple beers on the weekend at a barbeque or on holidays with family and friends. I mean heavily drinking.

Listen, God Loves People.

   As a matter of fact, the scriptures even tell us "to eat, drink and be merry" so I don't see things like drinking alcohol or eating certain meats as things deemed bad by Christ or as some sort of heaven wrecking offense punishable by God with a fiery sentence to hell. No, but to my brother who tended to drink and smoke more alcoholically and addictively than most, these enjoyments for some, left unbroke and unchecked can become bondage and begin to feel like hell on earth for others.

As a chain smoker for many years, he was sadly and unexpectedly diagnosed with sickle cell, terminal lung cancer at the age of 38 and his family and I had to let him go at 39.

   The day he died, lying on his back in bed at home, his body, skin and bones and his belly swollen, he asked me to read him two Psalms back to back, then he looked up and out into space and he said "Scott, he's here", I said, "Who is here Mark", he said "Squeaky sand", trying to follow I said, "Squeaky sand, no man, sand is crunchy sounding" and he began to laugh and said "That's what you think" and then in the most happiest and glorious way, he lifted his weak neck and head off the pillow, looked me right in my eyes and shouted in rapturous joy "I'm going to glory before you are" in the tune of nah nah nah nah nah nah. I said, "Alright Mark" and at that time I had been holding onto this vial of anointing oil in my pocket that I would use to anoint doorposts and pray for people and I felt prompted to anoint his whole body with it. So I poured it out into my hand and anointed his whole swollen chest and abdomen that afternoon with A Big Cross covering his whole torso and I said, "Mark, I have to go to work now but I'll be back tomorrow." An hour later, his youngest boy Corey called me and told me that his dad had just passed away.

In many ways, I believe his smoking and drinking hard liquor was his way of self medicating the emotional pain, traumatic memories and insecurities that he held deep inside. Mark had pain that needed a much deeper ministry and inner tending to than what any of us were equipped or able to administrate.

I do not believe God loved my brother any less when he was off the wagon than when he was on it, as if he loves us only when we are up but then disposes of us when we are down and out.

No, not at all.

Yet, I have seen this to be the sad indirect indoctrinations of many Christ confessing religious circles.

Personally, I believe such a view and teaching being taught can be a lot like deadly yeast being worked into the hearts of what may have become many mighty, young warriors for our Christian cause. This kind of yoke that says "Do this and don't touch that and you will surely be blessed but touch that and don't do this and you will be forever cursed" is not The Message Christ came to preach and gave his life for us all to hear and receive.

As a matter of fact, Christ's message was quite the opposite of that.

That blessed and cursed stuff was what Israel was under in The Covenant that Moses brought but not the freedom, grace, mercy, help and blessing that we as Christians have been given in Christ.

"So Christ has truly set us free. Now make sure that you stay free, and don't get tied up again in slavery to the law." ~ Galatians 5:1

Sometimes, I believe our religious yokes and lists of do's and don'ts can become so rigid and strict that many good men and women have died under the weight of condemnation and guilt of their own normal and innocent indulgences. Normal, simple, well disciplined enjoyments of life that have been turned into life condemning sins by strict religion.

Now, let me make it painstakingly clear that in no way am I wanting to underestimate the terrible, irreversible damage and consequences that become of poor decision making and a lack of self discipline in one's life. The aftermath, I have seen and experienced that comes from addictions like alcoholism, porn, gambling, greed and so on. When people agree and join with the wrong influences in their life, followed by an unresisted surrendering of their heart, mind, soul and will over to those deceptive influences is no laughing matter. Any amount of time in ministry, walking with people through such shipwrecks and travesty will bear quick witness that our enemy is alive and well and that he is still out there hijacking lives and driving people rampant to their own ruin, destruction and death.

So being careful here to not negate the seriousness of evil's agenda to steal, kill and destroy people's homes, families and regions, I am speaking specifically to these teachings and indoctrinations of religious groups that say in essence, you have to look like this, talk like this, act like this, be like this and you will be loved by God but fall short of what's on our list and we will all have to raise up a standard against you and banish you until you change…

This kind of approach, not done in love, can bring condemnation and kill people's zeal, hope and personal creative expression.

Although this kind of reasoning and logic that demanded the whole of Israel to adhere to The Law of Moses for them all to be blessed may have worked if you were an old covenant Jew born under the law in 30. A.D. but this same kind of logic does not translate well into our present day personal experiences of God's New Covenant Love, Forgiveness, Mercy and Grace.

Just ask anyone who has experienced Christ's Love and Forgiveness.

Public shunnings and standards set too high in church circles, I believe can actually work against the redemptive purposes and plans God has for His people and when we replace ancient scourgings and public stonings with modern day gossip and ostracizing, we appear to have never really come out from under the yoke and practices of that old way... Perhaps, we have made it a little less violent and a little more humane but the structural belief of having to earn God's goodness and blessing for the whole by our own personal adherence to the rules and then our need and practice to shoot our own wounded (even if that means it be ourselves) before these infractions or weakness of ours or others spread and get us all cursed. Well, this is the kind of logic and belief system that I believe Christ came and gave his life to set us all free from...

You See, The Good News is that The Anointing of Jesus came to break that old yoke and to bury that whole old system of holding one's trespasses against them.

Today, the message remains that by putting all of our faith in Jesus we receive The Holy Spirit of God who transforms us from the inside out and reveals us as who we really are. In Christ, we are revealed as reconciled children of God, no longer being charged for any of those infractions of the law that were committed by those born under the law.

Today, it is good to be born again into The Love and Grace of Christ.

You see, all of that Old Covenant stuff that was in The Law that condemned people for their sins (infractions of the law) were demolished and done away with, nailed to The Cross in 30 A.D. and that whole old system of death and curse for their sin was removed and made obsolete in

70 A.D. at The Siege of Jerusalem and the destruction of The Temple by Rome and was thankfully replaced by The New Covenant of God's love, mercy, forgiveness and grace... The New Covenant of Christ, that still remains for us all to this very day, revealing The Father's Heart, Love, Mercy and Grace.

The New Covenant came, removing the law and its severe consequences ushering in The Blessing, Help and Forgiveness of God.

And That's Good News!

Today,

"He has enabled us to be ministers of his new covenant. This is a covenant not of written laws, but of the Spirit. The old written covenant ends in death; but under the new covenant, the Spirit gives life."

~ 2nd Corinthians 3:6

Furthermore, Christ's message of God's Grace and Christ's demonstration of love and power comes to meet

us all right where we are, which for many growing up with
bad indoctrinations
may be feeling like doomed sinners.

Christ came, conquered death, set captives free and left us
His Holy Spirit to first convict us, yes of all our
wrongdoing but then to uproot from us any unloving and
offensive ways we may be carrying.

Christ teaches us how to be more loving to ourselves and
others.

He leads us and comforts us, he directs us and corrects us
and comforts us and embraces us and fills us with his
power so that we too are enabled to walk and be more like
Jesus on this earth, walking in a manner now
worthy of God's high calling and purpose for our life.

You see,

"God did not send his Son into the world to
condemn but to save the world through him."
~ John 3:17

In church life, when dealing with certain behaviors in
people that are very disruptive and insensitive to the well
being and peace of others let me not negate the very real

needed practice at times for Church discipline and as a minister, carrying a concern for the whole of those I minister to, I have personally had to ask certain people in our own gatherings to stop certain behaviors and after much fair warning and continued offenses, have even had to ask a couple individuals to leave our fellowship until they were able to get those things right in their life.

I am not ashamed of this and as a minister, I would do it again and again if need be but let me assure you that as a man who tries to practice long suffering grace with others, such discipline was implemented only after 2, 3 and even more had spoken repeatedly over and over again to these individuals about their on going offenses. This is never an easy thing to do and let me assure you that this was over some pretty serious stuff that I don't feel the need to mention here.

On the other hand, I have had people as well get on my case as a minister for not being harder on people for their sin. I have had to deal with people who seemed to want me to kick everyone out of the church but them. They were highly critical people who were fault finders, deeming everything they saw in people as wrong and sinful. These are people I like to call "Sin Cops." God Bless them but please for Heaven's sake, we don't need any more sin cops, we need merciful restorers to our fallen brothers and sisters in Christ.

So, with the need at times for church discipline noted here, let me return to the lesser things I have seen people ostracized for in religious circles.

~ Not believing tithing is a mandate for God's blessings.

~ Questioning certain eschatologies taught in the church.

~ Not subscribing to eternal conscious torment.

~ Seeing The Cross as atonement over substitution.

~ Not agreeing with the pastor on something.

~ Favoring different political views than the majority.

It's sad but true, that many have been asked to leave churches or treated like unbelievers under the allegation and accusation that by having differing views or beliefs than the majority they were causing too much confusion in The Church. As if the seeker was working for Satan to bring division and dissension, rather than seeing them honestly for who they were... believers, seeking truth.

Unfortunately, rather than seeing our brothers and sisters in Christ agreeing to disagree and moving onward in our God given mandates and commission, I have seen people figuratively "drug out of the church, stoned for having their own ideas and being left for dead in the parking lot" like The Apostle Paul (*See The Book of Acts*). I myself have personally received what some have coined as "The right foot of fellowship" a trend that seems to be happening more and more in congregations than what I'm sure Our Father in Heaven is pleased with.

When we have been hurt by a group of people and are forced to deal with such judgements of man, my very real concern is and always has been the very real disciplines of God because as far as I have seen, all that really comes out under the weight of man's own standards of righteousness being placed on others is broken and hurt Christians who came to church looking for help, love and acceptance and instead were judged, scorned, shunned and rejected.

On the other hand, when broken people come to God personally in an atmosphere of worshipping believers who know and represent His heart well, what is expected to come out is the condemnation people have already been living with for that particular weakness or unanswered questions they have and once they realize that they are still loved, then comes His Glorious Spirit, Grace and Power to strengthen them in their weakness and Christ himself to lead them into all Love, Healing, Freedom and Truth.

It is a beautiful, unexplainable work of miraculous deliverance, we get to witness in one another's lives, when we worship Jesus together regardless of our more trite doctrinal differences, wrong interpretations and personal judgments.

Chapter Twelve

Amazing Love

"He forgave us all our sins, having cancelled the charge of our legal indebtedness, which stood against us and condemned us; he has taken it away, nailing it to the cross. And having disarmed the powers and authorities, he made a public spectacle of them, triumphing over them by the cross."

~ Colossians 2:13-15

As an Ambassador of The Kingdom of God here on Earth with my citizenship in Heaven and as a minister of The New Covenant which is based on better promises than the first, this old approach of teaching law and adherence no longer applies. What I believe we need right now in this generation and future generations to come is a clearer theology that better equips us all on how to separate The Old Covenant of Adherence or Death, from The Glorious New Covenant of Christ's Spirit and Life.

The Grace, Love and Spirit of God that is still being poured out and being received by any who will simply believe and receive. Even Now.

In light of The New That has come, it is no longer a continual striving and fight on our part to adhere to a list of six hundred and thirteen commandments in order to be blessed by God. No, rather in Christ now, this becomes a surrendering and the inward transformation that takes place when we ask for and receive the work of God's Holy Spirit in our lives. This is The Way now and this is so much easier and so much more beautiful...

Yielding and submitting ourselves to The Holy Spirit of God in this way becomes less "I must be righteous before God" to "I am being made The Righteousness of God."

Listen, when we tell others what Christ has done for us, it releases his power to do it again in another's life. This is a powerful truth. It's a lot like how one would stack champagne glasses at a wedding reception in such a fashion that as the top glass keeps being filled it eventually overflows pouring down into all the others below. This is a beautiful demonstration of How God's Spirit fills us and how our testimonies of His love and faithfulness encourages others but let me also heed you that when our claims of freedom and healing become the whole of our testimony without any further relationship being built with the one who has freed us, we can unknowingly and unexpectedly be treading on dangerous ground.

In reflection of my own brother and countless others I have observed…

Let me explain.

Do you remember when the religious leaders in the bible were conspiring to have Lazarus killed because they were afraid of Christ's Dead Raising Miracle becoming known by more and more people and Christ's influence spreading any further than it already had?

The powers of darkness conspire in our lives the same way.

Listen, for example: When the whole of our testimony is based solely on our freedom from bad habits, as amazing and life changing as that act of God in our life may have been, I'm sorry to say that to others, such a story may not be any more impressive to them than let's say some well disciplined lifestyles achieved by devout practicing Hindus, Taoists or Muslims.

Ouch, and yes, I did just say that but let's face it, I know Muslims and Hindus who have overcome some stuff and adhere to strict dietary and abstinence laws more faithfully than some of our most devout Christians. So when we testify as Christians of how we used to drink, cuss, overeat, do drugs, or steal and lie and how now with God's help and grace in our life we don't do any of those things anymore, that's great and I encourage and live for such testimonies but my concern is that when we make these kinds of deliverances and miracles the whole of our testimony, without any real continued relationship with the one who freed us, when these sort of things become the end all of our whole testimony, our end in all, without any real reconciliation and further relationship being developed with God Our Father through the saving grace we have experienced in Christ The Son, I become deeply concerned that we are then only setting ourselves up for a very real calculated and strategic planned counter attack from the enemy, on our life and testimony.

You see, in our proclamations and boasts of Personal Righteousness, we can almost, if not careful, become stale matted, checkmated like a king, stuck in a corner by a couple of ruthless and persistent pawns.

After we get freed from something and have acclimated to our new found freedom and life, if we don't learn to remain fixed and steadfast in a continued relationship, at The Right Hand Side of God Our Father, like an eaglet nestled up under their Father's wing, we can easily, if not on guard, get caught off guard by the enemy, who is still prowling around like a hungry mountain lion looking for a baby bird to snatch up and devour.

So as True and Blessed as John 8:36 is;

"If the Son sets you free, you will be free indeed."

We must not forget;

"Stay alert! Watch out for your enemy, the devil. He prowls around like a roaring lion looking for someone to Devour. Stand firm against him, and be strong in your faith."

~ 1st Peter 5:8

Regardless of what the devil is doing to people all around you at school, work or even at church, "Stand firm against him and be strong in your faith."

It all reminds of a sermon I heard by T.D. Jakes where he pointed out what a poor decision it was for platoons of fighting men to bang on loud drums and wear bright red coats while marching out there in the middle of the woods during the Revolutionary War.

We must not be proud and full of ourselves but rather learn to stay humble and close to our deliverer, our healer, our redeemer, Our Father and friend. Over the years, it has become more and more clear to me that when Satan sees a way that he can destroy "Your Testimony" then he can try to discredit all of your claims of Christ's goodness in your life and trust me, this will become a strategic attempt by him and his diabolical cohorts to try and falter you.

Just think about this logically with me for a moment. To the alcoholic for example who says "God delivered me from alcohol", I believe that and let's say this newly freed prisoner then begins to yell it to everyone and their grandma from the rooftop as excited as any of us would be and they begin to exclaim "I haven't had a beer in 3 days, 3 months, 3 years or even 3 decades!" This is wonderful and I would never want to downplay this in anyway, I know personally, first hand that for an addict to get even one day clean under his belt is nothing less than a genuine miracle given by The Hand of God but then let's say at a family gathering, one afternoon when their resistance is low, the job has become mundane, the kids are driving them nuts and the dog just died, they decide to go ahead and have a cold one with their good ole Uncle Bob.

"Just one" they tell themselves after 1000 A.A. meetings have been telling them for years that even 1 would put them assuredly back in that hole of alcoholism and addiction deeper than they had ever previously known. So, having been successfully indoctrinated with that belief, they now find themselves feeling buzzed, scared, ashamed, confused and defeated, lost again trying desperately to drink to that belief systems dooming end.

They cannot see themselves as a normal person who simply had a beer because now they identify with being an alcoholic, deeply imparted with the belief that they are not normal like everyone else, and once they have failed in their sobriety, the only option left for them is to keep drinking more and more because that's what alcoholics do.

Thus, due to the indoctrination they have received and their experiences in the past, after that first beer, instead of calling it one, they find themselves closing the bar that night and opening the liquor store the next morning.

Now to the one who has no problem with alcohol, you may find yourself saying, "So what's the big deal. People like to go out and drink with their friends from time to time. It's a pretty common cultural happening", you might say "Not a problem for anyone as long as they don't make an unhealthy habit out of it." We may want to advise them to "Stop it now, get up tomorrow, take an aspirin, forgive yourself and get on with your moderate life again." Well, that may be simple for you or I to say but to the one who has made this abstinence the epiphany of their life and testimony. For the one who has told everyone that Jesus took from them their desire to drink, to then be found drinking again, for them the drink can become like the end of their testimony of Jesus and assuredly that's what the devil will assert on their heart and mind.

So what I am contending for here, is that if there has not been a deeper life commitment made to God after his amazing work and hand of deliverance and healing in our life, if a deeper relationship between us and the Father who has delivered us and healed us has not been cultivated… our conversion experience can become jeopardized and shallow at best.

Even in one of my favorite stories of The Bible found in Luke chapter 17. The one about the 10 lepers who were all cleansed and healed by Jesus, only 1 returned to give Jesus thanks. Now I'm sure the other 9 went about telling people of what The Lord had done for them but only one ever returned personally to give him praise.

If our healing and deliverance from whatever the case, is where our encounter with God has begun and ended, then our continued relationship with God has not been rooted and established and chances are, at this point, the enemy will return to attack you in that area and if he can get you to stumble, he knows he can get you to fall and with so much condemnation, guilt and accusation for that one simple drink or slip up, by the time he's done in your head, you may not even feel worthy of Christ's claim or love anymore at all. Especially if this behavior modification or abstinence was the whole and end all of your testimony.

Let me say it one more time for the sake of emphasis and please forgive me for being so redundant. If the whole of our testimony and ministry has been that God has delivered us from alcohol or anything else then the enemy will know full well that all he has to do is get you drunk again so he can destroy the whole of your testimony and by doing so, he will then want to come in again and again to continue destroying the whole of your life.

Now apply this same logic across the board to all drugs, vices, addictions, bad habits and the such. Apply this kind of thinking to the gambler, the smoker, the porn addict, the cheat or the scoundrel. One trip to the boat, one puff, one website, one slick manipulation, one little white lie and the whole of a person's miraculous redemption story has been proven false and all their claims of Christ and credibility have been flushed down the toilet in many people's eyes forever.

"So what is all of this expounding really about?" you may ask yourself.

Well for me, it has all been about pride.

Hear me out.

Many aren't aware of this but in antiquity, during the trying of the furnace process, the last impurity to come out of a crucible before a vessel could be deemed as pure gold was silver. Something many of us would still consider valuable and I believe that one of the last things we need to let go of in our own trying process is that very thing we have valued the most about ourselves. Perhaps it's your abstinence from things you used to do but no longer do or even things that you never have done and never will… It's still all about you.

Now, I'm not saying that this thing that you value about yourself is a bad or even good thing, in and of itself, it's just who we are using our greatest assets and even surrendering our weakness to and for... Ultimately, this is what I believe matters the most.

You see, the last impurity of all these lesser things that need to come out of us before we can all shine like gold in God's Kingdom, I believe is the final removal of our selfish pride. It's then and only then, that we can truly have all things in us, good and bad surrendered, yielded, corrected and ready, to be fully given to God.

Fully surrendered, having been tested, tried and proven true in the fire of affliction, a vessel coming out as pure gold, ready for Our Master's use.

With all things surrendered and yielded to Him, then our life can truly become all about Him and his purposes and plans for our life.

This is when those things we may have been using selfishly for ourselves become gifts that we have been given to Glorify God with.

We need to know that underneath everything else that has to come out first, that there is gold to be found in us that often only God sees and it's my belief that when He is finished with us, he wants others to see as well.

"Pride goes before destruction, a haughty spirit before a fall."   ~ Proverbs 16:1

For any who know or have known this kind of white knuckle living, suffering under the withdrawal of an addiction or the ostracizing of a religious group operating without any margin for error or grace. Let me just say, that I know personally how hard it can be with all of the religious guilt and condemning thoughts that come at us like arrows when we have been falsely accused, treated or indoctrinated. To be living under a yoke that demands perfection from a mean punishing God and people rather than receiving His helping hand and experiencing the grace of our yoke breaking compassionate Father. I want you to know God's learning curve and His Heavenly Assistance for you. I want you to know Christ's patient, long suffering, love, mercy and grace for you. I want you to know that Jesus is not against you but that he is truly madly in love with you and still for you.

If you have been delivered, Praise Him!

If you have received healing, Praise Him!

If you have been redeemed, Say it is so!

If you have been reconciled, Remain in Him!

And know that your journey in knowing and experiencing The Goodness of God in your life has really only just begun!

For Deliverance is only the children's bread, amongst a whole table that Our Lord has prepared for us.

Chapter Thirteen

Wonderful Feeling

We are almost there and the time is coming for me to tell what will be the hardest part of my story to tell but before I do, I wanted the heart of this book to leave you with this. Sometimes, I believe one of the best things anyone can experience in this life is to mess up. Yes, to mess it all up, to drop the ball and screw things up big, to fall short and to personally fail in our strivings for personal perfection and holiness.

Now, I'm not talking about premeditated sin or intentionally going out there and plotting anything evil. Absolutely nothing of that nature but to honestly and genuinely miss the mark on something we were going for and make a mistake.

To go for something and then see it crash and burn and to find ourselves humbly in that place where we need God to help us figure out how we are going to pick up all the pieces again. To experience that season where we are broken like humpty dumpty, shattered not knowing how all of the king's horses and all the king's men will ever be able to put us back together again.

To go through all of the heartache, guilt, shame and self defeat that comes with failing, only to come **Through it all** repentant, changed and realizing that you are still just as deeply loved and forgiven by God as you were before you tried and failed.

After experiencing a personal failure and then being able to turn our hearts back to God in Heaven and with his help, being able to pick up the pieces and get onward with our lives again. Only this time closer in our relationship with Him. Knowing and needing Him more. Needing His continued helping hand and leading in our life. With His Love and Wisdom helping us get our broken lives put back together again, while fighting our fears and pride that said it was something of our own merit that awarded us what was nothing more than His Good Grace.

To fall and fear His wrath only to be caught, corrected and held in a loving embrace of forgiveness and to know that despite your own hits and misses in this life, that you are still and always have been a continual hit with God.

To know that all of our fears, accusations and those feelings of inadequacy and the condemning thoughts you may have been suffering with for some time now, perhaps even years, were all in fact nothing more that mean old lies, that the enemy sent to keep you from knowing the truth, that you are God's Child and that he loves you dearly and that from God's heart and eyes, ***Through it all*** you have always been and never have been anything other than deeply loved and sought after.

Listen, the truth Church, is that Christians still and always will make mistakes.

I have not yet seen a person come out of the baptismal waters forever perfect in their performance or moral pursuits, myself included. What I have seen though, is that when I have fallen short of these man made or religious standards, I like many of you, have again felt utterly defeated, beaten down and even worthless again. Many times feeling as if I have been rejected and abandoned by God himself, and as if I wasn't worthy of His love or fellowship anymore.

The Good News is that those thoughts and feelings are all lies and simple strategies from an enemy whose goal is to try and convince us that we are anything other than still deeply and dearly loved children of God.

All of those onslaughts from the devil are just devil's fiery arrows and Satan's way of trying to once again take captive our minds and convince us that we are someone other than who we truly are.

Know this and stay in the light with this forever my friends and know that upon confession of these lesser things that have been tearing us up inside, there is always greater healing and freedom from those things to be had...

So, no matter what the case, no matter what you have done or how bad you have messed things up, know that you are still in fact, a deeply loved and cared about Child of God who He is willing to move Heaven and Earth for.

I want you to have peace, knowing God as Our Father like this...

It can be anything from drinking, pain killers, porn, heroin, crack, being late all the time or losing your temper. It can be working too much and not spending enough time with your kids. It can be a husband who hasn't been sensitive to his wife's emotional and spiritual needs or maybe a wife who hasn't been very sensitive to her husband's physical ones.

The correcting convictions of The Holy Spirit that are good and from God and the list of condemnations that are bad and from the devil can go on and on and I believe learning to spiritually discern between the two is key for our Christian growth and maturity. Whose unctions are truly The Holy Spirit genuinely coming to lead us and help us and whose naggings are just the enemy's mean accusations coming to beat you down and condemn you into a further descent of defeat, depression and failure.

The Holy Spirit and Spiritual Discernment is a gift and key in learning how to navigate these often hard opposing winds that try to alter our course.

The Apostle Peter whose own failings, like having denied even knowing Jesus three times to save himself a similar fate on The Cross, even before failing was told by The Lord;

"I tell you that you are Peter, and on this rock I will build my church, and the gates of Hades will not overcome it."

~ Matthew 16:18

When Christ himself becomes our foundation and when His Love for us becomes real, tangibly felt and experienced, regardless of all our failed attempts and constant struggles to get it all right and keep it all together, when we know that we are still loved even when we have dropped the ball and got it all wrong... Well, that's a testimony that God can really build something forever lasting on.

As long as we remain standing in the rubble of our past mistakes feeling condemned over and over again by a false standard or man made list of external do's and don'ts that God himself hasn't even placed on us and as long as we keep striving to obtain some place in our lives that holds no margin of error or grace along our way, I'm here to say, that we will still be operating more like slaves under the law of The Old Covenant in fear, than in This New Covenant as the forgiven and loved Children of God that we are in Christ, learning the ways of His New Covenant Grace, Power, Forgiveness, Help and Love that has been demonstrated for us by Jesus here on Earth.

Let me assure you, that no such list like the 613 commandments of The Old Covenant even exists anymore for any of us modern day believers in Christ and that all of the rules and regulations of The Mosaic Law and all of man's own made up religious do's and don'ts have all been done away with. Those condemnations that the enemy has tried to use against us over and over again, have all been nailed to The Cross at Calvary. It is Done.

It is Finished!

The sin that is between you and God and others was done away in Christ and now we can now stand free, to pursue without guilt, a personal and intimate relationship with Our Heavenly Father God who teaches us and trains us up, as a Father does, in the right way we should go.

As Christians here on Earth, with our faith in Jesus, having been reconciled to Our Father God in Heaven, we have His Spirit dwelling in us for our continued leading, strength, help, strong moral support and personal guidance.

He's a Good, Good Father!

I promise you, The Father, The Son and The Holy Spirit will never lead you wrong and His Grace is more than enough for whatever we are going through.

Bad theology and foundations can be found under the fallen ruins of anyone who has tried to build a house on anything other than the solid Rock of Jesus Christ himself. Jesus Christ himself is Our Rock. He is our Foundation. He has been faithful to us even when we have not been faithful to him. All our feelings of guilt and shame and all our fears of future failures and all of our regret from past mistakes and all of our present strivings can finally be ceased with this simple and profound, pure, simple, gospel truth.

You have been Forgiven and You are Deeply Cared for and Loved!

Will you receive that?

It is He who has begun this amazing work in you and He who is faithful to finish this work that He has begun. You are now His workmanship, so just learn to rest, relax and enjoy the process.

Let Him do and complete His work in and through you.

This is the difference between us trying to conform ourselves to some man made set of religious rules and regulations and us being transformed by The Raw Power and Love of God's Holy Spirit.

Another final truth to know and a hard lesson I have learned along the way is this... Jesus gave his life for that fallen brother and sister. Even when they have fallen. What I have come to witness and find as true, is that absolutely nothing in all of creation can ever separate us from the love that the Father and Jesus have for us all. Not even our sin and brokenness. I have asked people for years this stirring question. When the Hebrews were in chains and in bondage to Pharaoh and when they were freed and led out by Moses, were they any less Hebrew, in the chains, than they were when they were led out into their freedom?

People always say "No."

So I use this to contend love for all of my Christian brothers and sisters who are still chained up and bound by things. Their chains don't make them any less my brother or sister and they are not to be discarded and separated from us as much as they are to have their deliverance ministered to them by us.

Jesus has been given the keys and he gives those keys and authority to us as Christians. Please take a moment to ponder this truth and to drink deeply with me the verses found on the next page of this book.

"Can anything ever separate us from Christ's love? Does it mean he no longer loves us if we have trouble or calamity, or are persecuted, or hungry, or destitute, or in danger, or threatened with death? As the Scriptures say, "For your sake we are killed every day; we are being slaughtered like sheep." No, despite all these things, overwhelming victory is ours through Christ, who loved us And I am convinced that nothing can ever separate us from God's love. Neither death nor life, neither angels nor demons, neither our fears for today nor our worries about tomorrow—not even the powers of hell can separate us from God's love. No power in the sky above or in the earth below—indeed, nothing in all creation will ever be able to separate us from the love of God that is revealed in Christ Jesus ..."
~ Romans 8:35-39

You see,

Jesus loves us whether we are bound or free and yet, he wants us all free!

Whether we are rich or poor, yet he desires to see us prosper!

Whether we are healthy or sick, yet it is his will to heal us!

 Short or tall, skinny, overweight, right or wrong...

No matter what, nothing will ever be able to separate us from the love of God that we find in Christ Jesus.

No matter what our state is in even right now at this very moment, God's Love is present for you and remains available for us all and this isn't just an inclusive thing for Peter, Paul, John and other 1st century Christians.

 For God so loved the world...that he sent us Jesus.

His Love is revealed to us in Christ but being out of Christ does not negate His Love or make His Love obsolete either... I know this may stir some theological feathers here but hear me out on this.

His Love for you remains, whether you are to love him or not.

It's not even that we first loved Him but rather that he has chosen and first loved us. As recipients of God's Love being lavishly poured out on us... this is what I contend, needs to be the highest testimony we can proclaim, the love of God! God's Love! God Is Love!

Once fully realized, experienced and known, we now become experiential proclaimers of His Great Love! Having been filled, we can't help now but to speak of and overflow His Love! The Love of The Father and of The Son and of The Holy Spirit sent to redeem Earth and all of us that dwell therein!

Whether you know this or not, whether you have experienced His Presence or not, Jesus taught us that the way of His Father was to love others with the same love he has loved us with and to be good to all. Jesus even told us to Bless those that curse us and to Love our enemies.

We all have to know this. God loves us. All of us. Jesus gave his life for you and Christ's own life and power really is possible when The Father's Love for us all is flowing from His Heart to ours and then from ours unto others.

Especially those who do not know His Love.

I believe where many of us have got confused and misled about this, isn't in The Father or The Son's ability to keep on loving us. That is a given. God is Love. This is who He is and what he does. He so loved the world that he sent us His only begotten son Jesus in order to show us and demonstrate The Way of His Love. I believe where we get misguided is when Satan keeps trying to convince us that because of our failures and deceptions that we are no longer going to be loved by God. With all I have within me, I implore and encourage you:

Beloved, You Are So Loved, So Be Loved.

Before I return to my story, I want to press on through to you that God's love for us is granted but truly believing and receiving His Love for us... is a choice.

Today, I choose to have Faith in God's Love for me. Yes, the enemy likes to talk us into doing things and then he condemns us for doing them and yes he will keep trying to point his finger at you and highlight all of your "imperfections" and "weaknesses" and then tell you that God doesn't love you anymore because of them but I want you to know and I want you to be equipped now, able to *stand firm* against his tactics and lies and to know that no matter what, you are still loved by God. The devil is a liar and instead of agreeing with his lies about you and God, you can now start telling him the truth that it is actually in our weaknesses that God's Grace and Power is perfecting us.

"He said to me, "My grace is sufficient for you, for my power is made perfect in weakness." ~2nd Corinthians 12:9

In other words, as I like to say, God's Love keeps us and holds us close while Grace fills in all of those places we are still lacking and hurting.

"He arose, and rebuked the wind, and said unto the sea; Peace, be still. And the wind ceased, and there was a great calm."
                                        ~ Mark 4:39

We don't ever fall from grace, we fall into it.

We may fail but his love for us never does.

As born again believers filled with The Spirit of God having been given a New Nature in Christ that is now contrary to our old one. When we do fall short or move outside of God's love and will for us, it isn't any longer an issue about him not loving us. This has been established but I do believe our wrong doings and unloving actions do grieve Him. Of course they do. How can they not? Just as any loving parent would be grieved to see their children making poor and sometimes even downright dangerous decisions with their life. The Good News though is that as a Christian having been given a New Nature in Christ, to stay in any old darkness will not be possible.

The Holy Spirit has come to shine a light on all that darkness in our life and The Light of Christ will dispel all of it. He will not allow us to remain dishonest and hurt others without any conviction, rebuke and correction. As the scriptures correctly convey "The Lord disciplines those he loves" and this is actually a very beautiful thing. We truly couldn't do any of this without Him. He Fathers us and He will use all means to correct us and His correction in our lives should be feared, in a healthy way, as much as His correction should be valued. His love works through us and reproves us, corrects us and improves us.

Choosing to remain in His Love and seeking to stay in constant connection with His heart, direction and will for our lives is where God's fullness is truly experienced and found.

Outside of this truth and being deceived into believing "lies" that tell you otherwise is where the real danger lies.

"So humble yourselves before God. Resist the devil, and he will flee from you. Come close to God, and God will come close to you."
~ James 4:7-8

When we listen to devils that try and convince us out of the Love, Help and Grace that God continually has for us, this is where the enemy comes in and when he does, he is there to steal, kill and destroy.

Faith in God's Love for us tells us unceasingly that He is still with us and will forever be there for us, regardless of our grace covered mess ups along the way.

"Where sin abounded, grace did much more abound"
~ Romans 5:20

So Stay in Love. Another truth that I have come to know about Our Father God is that He sends The Holy Spirit when we ask Him to and when The Holy Spirit comes He not only comes with Power but He also comes as our comforter, our corrector, our wisdom and our guide. He is a teacher who will lead us into all truth and freedom.

"So if you sinful people know how to give good gifts to your children, how much more will your heavenly Father give the Holy Spirit to those who ask him." ~ Luke 11:13

A couple verses from Isaiah that I have come to rely heavily upon in my own freedom is found in chapter 30:20-21. They read as follows;

"Though the Lord gave you adversity for food and suffering for drink, he will still be with you to teach you. You will see your teacher with your own eyes. Your own ears will hear him. Right behind you a voice will say, "This is the way you should go,"
~ Isaiah 30:20-21

Today, as a believer and passionate lover of Christ, having grown up "outside of the box" not knowing all the religious denominations "do's and don'ts" and having learned in my wanderings to rest assured in the convictions of God and my own personal relationship with Christ, I know today, that if I am going too far to the right or to the left that I will be spoken to by The Holy Spirit.

This is one of the most awesome safeguards and most valued truths I have come to know about being a Child of God. We have a Father who isn't afraid to incline to us and say "No my child, this is the way."

Even more on point here, let's look at something Jesus himself told the disciples in John 15:10 *in* The Gospel of John's Red Letters;

"When you obey my commandments, (directions) you remain in my love, just as I obey my Father's commandments (directions) and remain in his love."

You see, it isn't that when we fail to obey that he stops loving us.
We have already established that but when we decide to not listen and decide instead to listen to deceiving spirits and follow foreign gods and other persuasive people rather than remaining in God's protective custody and love, I am sorry to say but will sternly say it, it is then, that we are

now treading outside of God's protection and into what can be some very dangerous and unforgiving grounds.

Outside of The Holy Spirit's directives and the land that God has predestined and prepared in advance for us to specifically walk in is where the enemy is roaming to and fro like a lion looking for whom he can devour *(See 1st Peter 5:8)*.

So the safest place for all of us as Christians, is to remain right here, right now, in the fullness and awareness of His life-changing presence, protection, love, wisdom, provision, guidance and grace.

This is the inheritance we have as Children of God.

He loves us, even when we fail, even when we make mistakes His love remains, and no, His grace isn't a license to sin, not at all… It is rather His helping hand and guidance along our own, often faltered ways.

So know this. God loves you no matter what and His grace reveals to us how intimately involved He is and how wanting and willing He is to remain in a committed helping relationship with us as his kids. He wants to help navigate us safely, despite all of our struggles, frailties, weaknesses and fears. All of those lesser things that surface and are getting skimmed along the way.

So now, finally before continuing on into the hardest part of my own story of failure and redemption, let me close this chapter with this.

When Jesus was asked in Matthew 22 what the greatest commandment in all of The Mosaic Law was, he actually replied with two.

He said;

"Love the Lord your God with all your heart and with all your soul and with all your mind.'This is the first and greatest commandment. And the second is like it: 'Love your neighbor as yourself.'All the Law and the Prophets hang on these two commandments." ~ Matthew 22:36-40

After many years of contemplation over this verse, I am safely able to arrive at this shore of a confident conclusion.

Unlike in "The Old Covenant" when "sin" was defined clearly as "any infraction of the law," I can boldly say today as An Ambassador of The Kingdom of God and as A Minister of The New Covenant that "sin" today can now be redefined as any infraction of love.

Love for God, Love for Ourselves and Our Love for one another.

This has become a solid and foundational truth for me. I can't say this has been taught to me by any man made religion or church doctrine but rather I believe revealed to me by The Spirit of God. My utmost and foremost goal today as a Christian is to remain in a constant awareness of His Love. Moving outside of my awareness of His constant continual love for me and others around me is to be missing it. I believe this is so important to know. Likewise, when we begin to move in accusation and condemnation of one another we are missing it as well. Even in the event of an individual's obvious sin and error. I believe our approach should come from a genuine place of redemptive, restorative correction and love rather than from a place of condemning judgement.

Now consider this. Right before Jesus went to The Cross to demonstrate and begin establishing God's New Covenant *of Love, Forgiveness, Grace, Restoration and*

Heavenly Assistance, He left the disciples with just one singular command that I have found to be the most important singular command to be found in all of the Holy Scriptures.

This one command, freeing the whole Nation of Israel from the 613 commandments they were under in Moses, unto this one singular command that Jesus gave the 12 at The Last Supper. Just before his crucifixion, descension, resurrection, ascension and enthronement as Lord over all, He bowed down low to wash His Disciples feet and left them with this;

"This is my commandment: Love each other in the same way I have loved you."
~ John 15:12

Then in John Chapter 17 Jesus prayed to The Father for all of us who would believe their message;

"My prayer is not for them alone. I pray also for those who will believe in me through their message, that all of them may be one, Father, just as you are in me and I am in you. May they also be in us so that the world may

believe that you have sent me. I have given them the glory that you gave me, that they may be one as we are one— I in them and you in me—so that they may be brought to complete unity. Then the world will know that you sent me and have loved them even as you have loved me."

~ John 17:20-23

Jesus clearly tells them to love others as he (Jesus) has loved them and then he clearly prays that the whole world would know that The Father loves us (you and me) just as he loves Jesus...

"Then the world will know that you (The Father) sent me and have loved them even as you have loved me."

~ John 17:23

We need The Holy Spirit to reveal this to us on a personal level and as well to The Church as a whole so that we can all know on a deep heart level that;

God Our Father loves us just as He loves Jesus.

My brother Mark made a noble decision to make his family first but the fruit that followed his decision leads me to the conclusion that somewhere in there some "lying devils" and "Bad Theology" may have taken captive his mind and led him down a road that I know wasn't God's best plan and outcome for his anointed life. I know that chain smoking cigarettes, firing up bowls of pot and drinking Irish Rose every day in the garage before he fell ill and died was not God's intended outcome and will for his life. I don't believe this is how The Lord would have written the last chapter in his life. Throw in all the hiding and lying about his relapse from his family because of guilt, brokenness and shame...

No, I do not believe this was God's will for my brother's life or any others for that matter. These are just not the kinds of outcomes that I believe Our Father predestines and wills for any of us.

By the time my brother was diagnosed with 4th stage lung cancer (caused by smoking) the doctors said he was terminal. For my brother's gifted life to have been cut short by the consequences that come from not remaining free in God's Love and to be deceived and allured into or away from his purpose and calling back into those kinds of expensive, unhealthy, devil inspired habits that made him sick is what the real trick of the enemy was. No shame on my brother. Forgiveness and correction on the teachings that put unloving and condemning doctrines of false perfectionism on people without allocating that margin of grace that God gives us all as we are growing and coming along. False teachings thus backfiring, making someones simple indulgence or slip into what can feel for the recovering addict (of all sorts) like a lifetime of failure and a permanent rejection by God and the fellowship. Especially when we have been taught that we have to earn our acceptance from God by a perfect performance rather than learning to receive His love, grace, help and acceptance of us... regardless of man's score cards.

I can almost see it now, how a demonic spirit of addiction and closely kin spirit of shame would have been high fiving each other on my brother's back, as he grew heavier and heavier, sicker and sicker, and more and more tired in that garage drowning his sorrows night after night with cigarettes, alcohol and pot. Trying to forget, after a hard long day of grinding out printing press gears in a machine shop.

Granted the labor of love. The sacrifice and cross that my brother carried day in and day out to keep his family sheltered, clothed, fed and provided for but for my brother Mark to have not seen his own kids weddings and his grandchildren... No, I do not believe that this was God's will or plan at all for him. For him to have died at age 39 with lung cancer, leaving a wife and two kids behind. No, I don't believe these sorts of things are God's Plan and Will. I believe that these are the kinds of dangers and outcomes we can face when we have been craftily allured and redirected out of it.

You see, the enemy knows that if he can attack someone's testimony, he can then have a chance at stopping their destiny. When he can discredit their claim of Christ's goodness in their life, he can then try to steal the plans and good works God still has in store for them.

This is why I always tell people that my highest testimony isn't about all of the unhealthy habits that I have been delivered from, which have been many and that you are about to hear about. My highest testimony isn't about being healed from a 20 year long incurable blood disease that I caught in my addiction that was chronically attacking my liver. It isn't just that I don't do this or that I don't do that anymore. I mean honestly, I still make mistakes in this life and on my best days, I will still probably fall short somewhere in thought, word or deed... So no.. My testimony isn't about becoming perfect or better than anyone else in my performance, discipline or character. No, if this was my only claim to fame, pride would surely come in and find me gloating right before my next fall.

No, my highest testimony actually doesn't have anything to do with my adherence to any self righteous or even man made religious rules and regulations.

No, my highest testimony is humbly of The Raw Love and Power of The Holy Spirit, come to give me a New Life and Nature in Christ Jesus. A New Nature who is constantly growing and maturing and who isn't comfortable in selfish, non-loving ways anymore and who daily needs Jesus and The Father's enduring mercy, kindness, grace and love to continually get me through...

The Holy Spirit literally being the air I breathe and the life I now live in Christ as a born again, Spirit Filled Child of God.

"I have been crucified with Christ and I no longer live, but Christ lives in me. The life I now live in the body, I live by faith in the Son of God, who loved me and gave himself for me." ~ See Galatians 2:20

My Highest testimony is of the love and help I receive from Our Father in Heaven as a born again Child of God and believer who has put all of my faith, hope, love and trust in Jesus!

Chapter Fourteen

Hurt

About the same time the band broke up so did my fiance and I. It was later a much regretted decision on my part. I was working all the time and had started developing a working relationship with a young lady who answered the phones at the pizza joint. She began to pursue me pretty seriously. So one day, I decided to break it off from Heather (my fiance) just to see what it would be like to go out with another girl. I guess some have called this kind of thing "cold feet."

Heather, my fiance at the time had been in a couple relationships before me but she was my first real love. I was 17 now and I guess just curious about other girls and just wanted to make sure that I wasn't missing out on anything else out there and this girl at work was really cute and nice. She had even remembered word for word a poem I had written, that really impressed me a lot. I fell for it. I told Heather that I wanted to break up and try seeing other people.

A couple months later, I went crawling back to her like a dog with my tail between my legs in the hopes of a reconciliation but it was too late. She had begun dating another childhood friend of mine. Her and Mike actually went on to get married and have been happily married ever since. God Bless them both.

So here I was now, my dreams of "Rocking The World With The Word" were gone. My girlfriend and fiance of 2 years was gone and now without any weekly Bible Study, Christian fellowship and all accountability gone....

It didn't take long before I was gone.... Remember?

"Where there is no vision, the people perish..." ~ Proverbs 29:18

Like a perfect storm everyone around me began partying and drinking more. Instead of going home after work, I started going to house parties and bonfires in the woods. I was looking for a sense of belonging and wanted to be around my friends all the time. I completely stopped reading The Bible and writing and it wasn't long at all before I took my first hit of weed. When I found out Don (our singer) and 2 other of my best friends were smoking, I just gave in and decided to give it a try and I found that the effect pot had on my over active brain waves was pretty amazing. Already being the very high strung and wound up tight inside kind of guy that I was, pot was like a sedative that actually worked and seemed to bring me down to a level I enjoyed and wanted to stay at.

I also started drinking Captain Morgan and popping Tylenol pm's. I guess to avoid feeling anything anymore. All I wanted at this point was to be comfortably numb. It was like I had found the perfect combination to slow down the overactive thinking and musing and was finally able to rest all of the racing, wearying thoughts that had been keeping me up at night. A restlessness that had pretty much plagued me since being a child crying in that bed.

I was all of a sudden coming home every night to my mom's house drunk and high and as you could imagine, this started some horrendous yelling fights between us.

In hindsight, I'm sure she saw me as going down the same road she had witnessed my brother stumble down some years earlier and her way of correction has always been to try and bully people back on track. Statements like "I brought you into this life and so help me God, I can take you out of it" and "If you don't stop it right now, I'm gonna knock you into next week" were words I heard quite frequently growing up. Unfortunately though, the threats of locking me out of the house or saying she was going to call the police on me had more of a backfiring effect than what I'm sure she had intended. Such anger, rage and threatening only seemed to reinforce my self medicating. When I was sober, her yelling and verbal jabs always seemed to hurt me emotionally quite deeply. When I was intoxicated it didn't seem to matter anymore what she would say. She could say things like "You don't love and respect me." and instead of this hurting me and making me angry inside, I could just go and smoke another bowl and not even seem to care anymore.

At this point, I didn't even know what I was living for. If I wasn't going to be marrying Heather, writing lyrics and playing drums in a band that was going to bring The Good News of Christ and His Kingdom to the world, if I had lost all direction and no longer had any of the above to keep going on for. It was like I had lost all zeal and hope in my life. All I wanted to do now was self medicate and escape all of these disappointments and shattered dreams that had so abruptly become of my life.

To make things even worse, I was 17 about to turn 18 years old and according to my mom and dad's divorce contract, it was now time for my mother and I to lose our home. So as a child, I internalized that this all somehow had to be my fault. For children trying to process adult resolutions it is easy sometimes for them to do this, to believe that things are their fault that actually are not. In my young reasoning, if I hadn't turned 18 my mom would have never had to lose her home. This was not an easy thing for her and even to this day, 24 years later, she still speaks of when she had to lose her home. Before the move, she used to wake me up on Saturday mornings and make me go, all hung over with her to look at apartments and mobile homes. I really was not in any shape to go anywhere at this time and I was really of no help at all to my mom at this time in my life. Working and partying after work had become a full time job for me and there wasn't much left of me after that. I'm sure she would have liked a much more supportive son at this time in her life but I just wasn't there mentally or emotionally.

Through it all, like a good functioning addict though, I somehow managed to hold down my job at the pizza place. One of the good things about starting work at 3:30 in the afternoon was that at midnight when I got off, I could go straight out partying with my friends. We spent a lot of nights at Denny's smoking bowls in the parking lot and drinking coffee until the sun came up. It was the place to go when no one else was having anything going on. I was sort of wandering around from place to place at this time and I just totally got swallowed up by that whole subculture of metalheads, goth rockers, punks and potheads. At this time, I remember wearing a plaid suit (I had found at The Salvation Army) with a pair of black combat boots. I had flamingo pink liberty spikes that stood a foot off the top of my head. I had my eyebrow, both ears, my tongue and lip pierced and my appearance turned heads everywhere I went. I'm not sure if it was for attention or what but I did sort of like the way my anti conformist attire would make heads turn when I walked into a place. I had learned enough by this time about how much of our world works to know that I was happy to be setting myself apart from it. Drinking and smoking and laughing with friends continued to escalate until LSD came around and I experimented with it more than what any sane person probably should have. As I mentioned earlier, my late nights kept getting later and later and I would usually come home crashing into my mom's place a little after dawn and then sleep it off until I had to go back to work again. At the pizza place they called me Chief. I did a lot including steak sandwiches, rib dinners, chicken dinners, soups, salads and more... I was good at my job but as my partying escalated and my peer groups diversified, my mom's patience began dwindling and her concerns for my well being continued to grow.

Our arguments became more and more enraged. She wanted me to straighten up my act and I just wanted her to leave me alone and mind her own business. It got so bad that I eventually began sleeping in my car in the parking lot where I worked to avoid any conflict with her. A tactic I had learned watching my dad hide out at Dunkin Donuts years earlier. I can remember the owner's son coming out and waking me up at 3:00 pm for work everyday. It was great, I got paid there, I could eat there and now I could even sleep there! I had all I needed for a life pursuant to continual drug and alcohol induced bliss. I had all I needed to keep my weekends fueled with whiskey, Marlboro's and pot.

What more did a young disillusioned man like myself need?

At one point, the owner's sister, who I had worked with for years in the kitchen gave me money to go take a shower and get a hotel for the night. I guess I had unknowingly began to stink a bit but in my condition wouldn't have even noticed. Things for me were already pretty bad but in my broken and hurt little world, I believed it was all good. I mean after all, I was still working, I had friends to drink and smoke with every night and I was avoiding all confrontation with my mom. So at 18 years old, in the summer, shortly after my mom had lost her house, I was sleeping in my car, while my mom put down on a new mobile home in a place called Sterling Estates in Justice IL.

By this time, I had stopped going to see my dad on weekend visitations because he had recently moved with his wife across the country to Park City, Utah. His job had an opening that required him to move to Park City. I had the opportunity to be flown by him for one month in the summer to see this incredible place on Earth. Keep in mind now that I'm from Chicago, so the mountains had me humbled, awestruck and wrecked. They were breathtaking to me and I remember for the first time, after drying out a bit, how small I was amidst those massive mountains and I remember more than anything being without a girlfriend for the 1st time in 3 years and how much I hoped to have a good woman again to love and be by my side while taking in all of that beauty. As I hiked in those mountains, I remember longing for someone who would believe in God and who I could share those feelings of His Majesty with.

I longed and asked God for another chance at love.

From my wounded side of things I had begun to believe that much of my problems with Heather and my mom was because of my inability to do or get anything right in this life. Even as an adult, I still sometimes have to deal with this and wrestle with a deep rooted lie inside that tells me that "I'm not good enough."

My mom had been pretty hard on me since my dad left and she would yell things at me over and over again like "You don't love or respect me" and I can't even put into words how deeply wounded and hurt I was as a child being told stuff like this. I had begun to believe at one point that everyone around me would end up suffering unhappiness and eventually leave because of me. I ended up internally blaming myself for just about all things bad in my life. Somehow, like through some demonic filter, words, thoughts and events would get twisted in my mind and find ways to make me the reason for all of the unhappiness in my mother's and others life. At one point, after being ranted and raved on for hours and hours on end, I decided to take a whole bottle of tylenol pm and I ended up in the ER at Christ Hospital in Oak Lawn. After I was released, I remember feeling really, really heavy and my mom putting a movie in the VCR called "Heaven's Gate, Hells Flames."

As my addictions and dependency deepened, doctors eventually diagnosed this kind of thinking and deep self hatred as Clinical Depression.

I know my mom has always meant well and that her heart is good but she has been telling me ever since I was a little boy that I didn't love or respect her. She still tells me this even to this day. I have been badly indoctrinated for almost 4 decades with the accusation and belief that I am a horrible person who doesn't even love or respect his own mother.

Today, I know on a certain level, that this is not true and that I have done all I can to show my Mother true love and respect but the truth is that she is the one that believes her own "lies" about herself and others. The lie that no one loves her and this has now unfortunately become a similar lie my own life has had to contend with. The lie that I am no good and unworthy of anyone's genuine love. I guess I learned it by watching her in a way.

I am learning today the truth of God's love and his kindness expressed one unto another through one another and if it wasn't for the help of my wife and kids and our healthy friendships with spirit filled believers, I really don't know where I would be today other than lonely, defeated, addicted and most likely dead.

By this point in my story, I am 18 years old and after flying back home to Chicago, I have decided to start drinking again and drop out of my last year of high school. I'm still working though, like a good functioning alcoholic does, still partying hard at night with my friends and thinking everything was good and then another unexpected tipping point happened... I lost a friend of mine.

His name was Matt. He was a really great kid. He was from Southern California. We all called him California. He was such an exuberant character and his personality was a lot like the west coast. Always bright and shining. He was dating one of my friends. One evening, Matt spent the night at my mom's new mobile home with me. I remember telling him all about Christ's love and how he wanted to live in our hearts and minds and he totally got it and he was all smiles about this. We asked Jesus to come into his heart and live there and it was genuine, his prayer and acceptance of Jesus was real and he was all excited and lit up over this. He had a bunch of questions and I did my best to answer all that I could and I was lifted for a moment to have been given the opportunity, in light of the more recent downward spiral I was on to still be able to share this gospel truth of Christ's desire to be with us, for us and in us.

The next day, I drove him home and he said that he would page me later. That evening, I got a page from him asking me to come pick him up and take him to a party at another friend of ours apartment in the next town over. I was all ready to go and on my way out the door when my mom stopped me and demanded that I put together this small entertainment center she had just bought. I was so upset about having to do this but I submitted or else I might not have had a place to peaceably sleep that night.

Matt told me that he had found another ride to the party and that we could catch up later when I was done. That evening some turn of events happened and I had the opportunity to go out with some other friends of mine and

I never made it to the party that night. The next day, I got a phone call from Julie, his girlfriend, telling me that Matt was dead, she told me that he was murdered.

Time stopped, as it does, when we hear these kinds of things and I could hardly believe what I was hearing. Apparently, him and another young man from the neighborhood got into a bit of a drunk and stoned fist fight in the parking lot of that party. While they were getting out of a car, I guess Matt had accidently shut the car door on the foot of this kid Randy and a fight broke out between the two of them.

Randy was a local gang banger and I heard that Matt (California) was actually getting the better of him, fist to fist, when Randy pulled out a 6 inch pocket knife and began to stab Matt. Several times, he stabbed Matt, a total of 14 times in his chest, stomach and ribs. Another friend of ours, Tony threw his bleeding body into his car and rushed him to J.J. Peppers, a local liquor store on the corner of 79th and Roberts Rd.. At the store they called an ambulance as Matt continued to bleed out in his car. The story goes that with a punctured heart and a collapsed lung he died in surgery 3 and 1/2 hours later.

I was so struck down and couldn't believe any of this was happening. If you had known Matt you would understand. He was the sunshine. It didn't make sense to me that of all the people that could have been taken, that California would be gone.

At Matt's wake, a week later, all my friends were placing things like a bottle of Jack Daniels, packs of Newports and rolled joints into his coffin and I just kept thinking "Isn't this the reason he's dead right now?"

I had heard from another gang banger who was a friend of Randy, that he was withdrawing from Heroin when he went off and stabbed Matt.

"Heroin", I thought to myself… that hadn't even been heard of around any of us until now.

I had come a long way from being encircled by kids with open bibles and pure hearts to all night parties, self destruction and now even murder. I was now surrounded by kids on drugs, drop outs, some who were in gangs and I had just experienced what I will call my first major drug induced loss.

I recall thinking to myself, "If Matt had only known many of us just one year earlier and if our ministry would not have come to such an abrupt crashing end, if he was learning the scriptures with us every Tuesday and

Thursday night pursuing a good, clean life in Christ, if all of us were still gathering together to get into the word of God and gathering together to pray for each other and to confess our weaknesses to one another and to hold each other accountable instead of gathering around each other to get obliterated, high and drunk... I believe there could have been a much better chance that Matt would still have been here alive with all of us today." It's a touchy place for me to go into and an underlying pain and brokenness that remains... Yet, to this day I still use it often as a Minister.

Many times as a minister I have sat with a group of youth and told them Matt's story. I explain to them at 12 and 13 years old that experimenting with drugs is a lot like sitting around a table playing Russian Roulette with your best friends. The game of passing a gun around with one bullet in the chamber and people placing it to their own head and pulling the trigger in hopes that they don't get the loaded chamber. In this game, some eventually, sooner or later, die a pretty brutal death. I tell the kids that the drugs people are messing with may not end up getting everyone at the table but that you can count on it getting some. I let them know that the end result of drug abuse will be the life long battle and struggle of some and the inevitable death of others and then I ask them to look around the room at each other and ask themselves the question. "Is there anyone in this room right now that you would be willing to play this game with?"

The night of Matt's wake didn't do anything good for my depression either and I ended up medicating the only way I knew how. I got seriously drunk and hung out with this pretty girl named Kim. I had seen her around school several times and I had partied in some of the same circles with her, so after indulging in large amounts of pot and Vodka, while reminiscing Matt's life together, we ended up becoming pretty good friends. I guess you could say we were there to help each other cope but it would probably be more accurate to say that we were there more to help each other dope.

Another night after Matt's death we all found ourselves gathering to drink, smoke and mourn the passing of the late great Jerry Garcia of the Grateful Dead. All I know and remember is that we were at a park getting all tore up and wasted when somehow I ended up consummated with Kim in a pullout bed at my friend John's apartment. I liked Kim, I liked her alot but I don't believe sex would have been the outcome that evening if there was no drugs and alcohol involved. Remember, I was a shy kid and I didn't have any moves.

I remember Kim being a lot like I was in high school. She was very quiet and defiant. The next evening, after we had intoxicatedly sealed the deal, she and I sat in my car in a local Jewel Osco (Convenient Store) parking lot, drinking more whiskey, smoking more pot and while talking about Matt and Jerry's death, I began to dream about them beautiful mountains I got to see at my dad's house in Park City Utah and how much I wanted to be able to share them with someone else. I was high, as usual and I had 60 dollars to my name and on a strange whim, I asked her if she'd like to take a road trip with me. She said "Sure, where are we going?" and after telling her about the mountains, I drove her to her mom and dad's place down the street and this is exactly how it went. I walked in having never met her parents before and I stood in the front doorway while she charged through her house and said "Hey mom, this is Scott, I'm going across the country with him", she then stormed into her bedroom and came out with a couple pillows and a garbage bag filled with some clothes and said "Come on let's go", I looked at her mom sympathetically who looked at me shaking her head as if she had been through this kind of thing with her before and I said "Nice to meet you Ma'am" and me and Kim were off from Chicago down I-80 West with Tom Petty's Wildflowers playing on a boombox in the backseat.

We had enough pot to make our way at least halfway across the country and then we ended up meeting some kind people who owned a little diner and hotel along the way who graciously fed us and put us up for a free night. A trip that should have taken us 22 hours took us a bit longer on our first trek west and it was all very freeing to just get away from what I thought was a lot of madness and confusion going on among my peers back home in Bridgeview Il.

When we finally got to Utah, we were honestly in a really bad mental, emotional and spiritual state. Our brains were totally polluted with all of the wrong logic and pop culture. In so many ways, we were emulating that era's darker art. All the wrong art. Her favorite movie and soundtrack was "Natural Born Killers" and my favorite bands were Morphine, Nine Inch Nails and The Velvet Underground. Art that was fueling our addictions rather than deterring us from them.

My dad and his wife were nice enough to set us up in a spare bedroom and when we got there, we continued to party. I had called and told "Don" our old singer (who had recently received an inheritance at 18 years old from the death of his biological father) what was going on with us and he decided to wire me 500 dollars which I was able to buy a lot of Rolling Rock, pot and whiskey with. We would get stoned, drunk and lost driving around in the mountains of Utah. It all seemed like a pretty good time until my dad started putting pressure on me to find a job. He pretty much demanded that if I was going to stay and make a life for myself and this girl in Utah that I was going to have to man up and find a place to work.

Now, I had just completely walked away from my job at the pizza place in Justice IL. like a jerk with no fair warning and for me to find another job at this point.... Well, I just really didn't want to do this anymore. At this point, working would have messed up my drinking schedule. All I wanted to do was drink and stay high. So naturally, when work and finding jobs was being pushed on us, this is when we started missing all of our good, non working, partying friends back home in Bridgeview.

We may not have realized it at the time but we were addicts who were just using people for a place to crash and stay high. So one night, me and Kim got to talking and I said "Hey, what if we were to go back to Chicago, I'll get my old job back at the pizza place and we can get an apartment together." She was really into this idea and as I talked about it she was already decorating the place in her mind. It was going to be our all out party pad, decked out with cold beer in the fridge, colorful graffiti on the walls and black lights everywhere. All of our friends would be welcome at any time and if they ever got too lit they could just sleep on our floor. It would be our safe place, where everyone could fall. A place for everyone who had no other place to go. This was the plan and the new vision. So with no real thought or concern of how this may upset my dad, we quietly packed up our car, snuck it out of the driveway and in the middle of the night, we were off again... Sweet Home Chicago.

Chapter Fifteen

Us and Them

I'm 19 years old now, I'm back in Chicago with my old pizza job back and we are on a mission to create a place where all of our pot smoking, acid dropping and whiskey drinking friends could go and party safe without getting hurt or killed like Matt. Good intentions with a path paved straight to Hell.

You see, as you can imagine, many of us were not always on the best of terms with our parents at this time. As a matter of fact, when Kim and I got back to Chicago and we put down on our apartment, my Mother wouldn't even step foot in it. She stood outside of our place and called it "A den of iniquity."

As I had said, in a previous chapter, my friends over the years had become many of the ones who felt like outcasts in our society and who many times may have been shunned by the greater good. I mean, I had one friend from the trailer park whose dad once beat him with a belt attached to a steel buckle for refusing to drive to the Westside of Chicago to buy him crack.

So our front room floor did in fact become a big sleeping pad for many drunk, addicted and homeless kids. I remember breaking out a quarter pound of pot on our kitchen table and telling everyone in the apartment to roll themselves up a big Bob Marley before weighing it, bagging it and getting it ready to distribute.

We smoked a lot of pot! A real lot! After 6 months in this place our walls were yellow. I can remember passing a bong around and being handed a bowl, passing it around and being handed a blunt, passing the blunt around and being handed a joint and so on....

Somewhere in the midst of all of this partying me and Kim had become quite the drug buddies and even decided that it would be a good idea for us to get engaged. I'm not sure what her real feelings were on getting married but once again for me, with my Christian upbringing, I could at least not have to feel guilty anymore about being in a sexual relationship with a girl I wasn't planning on marrying.

You see, by nature, I have always been a very loyal person. I don't cheat on people. So committing to her wasn't an issue for me and if it wasn't for drugs, we may have still been together to this day. The fact of the matter though, is that these drugs that drew us together, were the same drugs that later ended up tearing us apart and I'm just grateful today, that neither of us died or had children before they did.

These kinds of things are always harder when kids are involved.

Up until this time, Kim and I were really quite the rock-n-roll, metal-head, goth, hippy punks. I was coming from a real heavy rock background and we both were very experimental with the earthy stuff, trying to find enlightenment of some sort through Jim Morrison lyrics, pot and weekend long LSD trips. We had both grown up listening to 60's music and we were both into the ideology of peace and love and that's when it began to happen, another tipping point caused by heavier substances finding their way into our local party pad.

Drugs other than pot, alcohol and the occasional hallucinogenic showed up. Some of the local gang banger kids from the trailer park that my mom had moved into, started coming over to my apartment and they would sprinkle cocaine on the weed we were smoking and it was no time at all that we were all sniffing it up our noses.

What a quick, even more downward spiral that became. I used to tell people that my life was like a series of hitting bottoms and then looking for a shovel.

The first time I rode what they call in Chicago "The Heroin Highway" it wasn't even to get heroin. I knew better than to ever touch that stuff. The first time I ever rode out to the Westside of Chicago was to get what they called "Pony Packs" of raw powdered cocaine. We loved how it made us feel when we rolled it in our weed and snorted the stuff. We could stay up all night and day drinking and getting high now. Cocaine became so popular so fast and everyone around me wanted me to keep going to get more of it for them. I mean it was like 24/7 people were asking me, "Can you get me some coke?" A friend of mine (one of the gang affiliated friends) who was more acquainted with the drug trafficking scene in Chicago than I was, showed me how I could easily get more anytime I wanted. Day or night. All I had to do was jump out of my car at certain known intersections in the ghetto, run into a hidden gangway and tell the guy serving the stuff "One Time." One time would get me 10 dollars worth, "Two Times" 20 dollars worth and so on. Many of the young people who were coming to my apartment now on a regular basis (more and more everyday) were afraid to go into those parts of the city, so they would pay me to do it. The West Side of Chicago had a pretty bad reputation for itself in the early 90's and young suburban white kids weren't encouraged to go anywhere near it. So me, already having been made familiar with how these drug purchases were easily made and having grown up with and not being afraid of black people, I was the one being elected and paid to go...

I would double all the money. I would get everyone 10 dollars worth of pot or coke for 20 dollars and this would leave me and Kim with a free bag of either, every time I got anyone anything. I can recall having let's say 100 dollars in one pocket for this guy, another 50 in another pocket for her over there, 100 more in a third pocket for those 2 over there and so on...

I could easily be riding out into the city to get 5, 10, 20 bags or more (felony possession of a controlled substance) knowing that when I got back, my fiance and I were going to be getting half of all these peoples drugs. As you can imagine, the party for me and her never stopped and we are both very blessed to still be alive. We had people knocking on our bedroom window at 2:00 am in the morning wanting me to go get them more coke.

So here I was, riding out to get weed and pony packs every day for all of us young drug addicts in the community....

God have mercy on me.

That's when this kid we all loved named Skater Paul, the same guy who showed me where to get this stuff, who was as well a gang member from the trailer park and the same guy who told me about Randy (Matt's Murderer) being on Heroin, comes walking into my apartment one evening and says these life changing words to me.

Our conversation went as follows;

"Hey Scott," he said. "You really like getting stoned don't you?"

I said "Yeah" and he said "Do you want to get stoned to the 10th power?"

I said "Sure."

Then he laid out this brown colored powder on my kitchen table called Karachi.

Now up until this time in life, all I had known about Heroin was that it was something you'd have to stick a needle in your arm for. I had never heard of Heroin that you could sniff up your nose like Cocaine. It was commonly known in Chicago as China-White. He laid a line of it out on my table that night and it was similar looking to coke but had a browner tint and it was a very rare and potent form of sniffable Heroin that had been smuggled in from Pakistan. Intrigued by his proposition to get stoned to the 10th power and already being inebriated with my defenses and inhibitions down... before I even really knew what I was doing, I grabbed a straw from the table and did what was probably the worst thing I could have ever done to myself.

I did my first line of blow.

Kim followed suit right behind me and so did a few others at the kitchen table that evening, an evening that years later I would be weeping and pleading God's Forgiveness for.

You see, I was always wanting to "Be Down" and that evening began a downward spiral for me and others who some have never made it back from and this still leaves a deep hurt and unresolved hole in my soul.

There are no words for this. Only hurt.

Again today, when giving kids my Russian Roulette speech, I tell them that some may try drugs and not like it and stop them. Some may try them and like them but as soon as the drugs start causing problems at home, in school or in life they'll stop. Some may try them and do it in moderation and use these things more recreationally and never really get hooked or too badly addicted... but then I tell them that the sad remaining remnant of them who play this game will die or spend a lifetime wasted and struggling as addicts.

I tell them with emphasis that the inevitable truth is that these drugs at some point, sooner or later, will get and kill some of them sitting at the table.

I tell them this from personal experience.

I let them know that by experimenting with drugs you are in fact passing around a loaded gun that will sooner or later end up getting some people killed and after it does, it will get another and then another and as long as you keep reloading that gun and playing, it will keep killing them. Then I like to point out that if you are one playing this game that you will never really know when or whether or not it's going to be you next or your best friend sitting next to you.

You see, I never thought that it would be me that this stuff would get but to date, I have died and been revived several times due to unexpected drug overdoses. It's only been by God's Grace and a praying mom at home, I'm sure, that I am even alive today and able to tell you this story.

People say that every drug addict has their primary drug of choice and the night I sniffed Heroin for the 1st time, I had undoubtedly found mine and unfortunately, so did a few others in the room that night.

I quickly became a bonafide Heroin addict.

I wanted as many bags of that stuff as I could get up my nose everyday all day. One of the other gang member Heroin addict kids, who started making it over to our place, out of the kindness of his young and addicted heart, tried to warn me about it and even told me "Whatever you do Scott, Please, never do it 2 days in a row."

He was genuinely trying his best, already being addicted himself, to warn me. His name was Slim and to this day, I remember that conversation and honor him for that fair warning but by then it was already too late. I was hooked as fast as I had experimented with it and before I knew it, everyone around me was doing it as well. It was like a whirlwind from hell that swept through our community, like a child stealing tornado. It was like a black plague that came into our region, killing and destroying many good kids, families and homes.

For us as addicts, it was like devils themselves literally taking control of all our young minds and wills and trying to run us all to our early deaths. We had been taken captive, without any of us wise enough to see it coming or the power within strong enough to resist it.

I have often likened Heroin addiction unto devil possession and what it would be like to be a hijacked car. It was like having "a spirit of addiction" jump into the driver's seat of your life and grab the wheel wanting to crash and kill you and hurt everyone else around you.

Within one year's time of shrinking back from being a young on fire Disciple of Christ and playing drums in a Christian Rock band with my older brother, I was now being taught by Satan Disciples how to obtain and ingest massive amounts of drugs and darkness into my mind, soul and body, trying to medicate my feelings of loss, hurt, confusion and restlessness.

I was now chemically dependent.

I was so deceived, broken and vulnerable and the delicate balance of chemicals in my brain had now been altered and set off kilt by all of the outward substances I was putting into my mind on a daily basis trying to make myself feel right again. My tolerance grew very quickly. What started out as 2 bags a day became 3 bags a day and so on and before I knew it, I was sniffing up to 5 or 6 bags a day and I found myself out at night with other Heroin kids yanking car stereos out of cars to resell in the morning and stay high.

I had never been a thief, I had never stolen anything from anyone until I had become a Heroin addict but after that "spirit of addiction" got its claws in me, nothing else seemed to matter anymore.

Nothing mattered other than getting Kim and I our daily quota.

Kim stayed home a lot and waited for me to get back with the stuff. It got bad for us both really fast. It's the nature of these kinds of drugs. Every day now for us became about getting enough Heroin up our noses to avoid the withdrawal that would come if we didn't.

If we didn't get X amount of bags in our system, we would begin to get really sick, emotionally, physically and mentally.

We later learned that Randy, who had killed my friend Matt, a year earlier, had just been sentenced to 20 years to life and was actually friends with all of these kids who were now filling our apartment and it was all just descending and going bad and down for all of us so fast...

Then more LSD came into the picture and not so much for the occasional "spiritual enlightenment" but more like for the challenge to see who could do the most.

This became totally nuts. I can remember one evening dropping 3 black and gold pyramid gel caps, sniffing 2 bags of heroin, smoking cocaine laced pot and then smoking a wicky stick. This was a cigarette dipped in some very potent embalming fluid.

I have often wondered how we had got away with such craziness without ever once having the local authorities called on us. I mean one of the local "Hoodrats" (as the gang members in our region were being called) tagged large gang symbols over my door and on the stairway of the apartment building we lived in and still no one ever called the police on us. Sometimes, I honestly wondered if the neighbors were scared to say anything or if they were all just really understanding and empathetic about the young kids hooked on drugs partying downstairs all the time.

Either way, that night I remember sitting next to my band's old 800 watt PA system turned up loud enough to rattle the pictures on the walls and as I melted listening to the words "Bye, Bye Blue Skies" by Pink Floyd I remember becoming unable to speak. It was like a dark cloud had come over me and covered me and while I could still see everyone around me and I could hear them talking about me, as if they were all concerned... I couldn't speak a word.

It was like I had become a prisoner within myself and although my eyes were wide open and I was sitting upright looking out at everyone, I couldn't speak or express myself to anyone. Brandon, a good friend of mine was partying with us that night and I remember him looking me straight into my eyeballs like he could still see me in there somewhere and telling everyone "Don't worry, he's going to be okay". He doesn't know this but those words were actually very comforting to me that evening because I really wasn't sure myself anymore. If you ever read this? Thanks Brandon.

Here's what needs to be noted though and what I still find amazingly alarming. From that very hard partying evening on, I was plagued with what doctors would later call a severe anxiety disorder. What's amazing to me, is that I could actually remember "feeling the moment" when that anxiety set itself in for the first time and took its roots in my mind and soul. It was literally like "a devil" taking up it's tormenting residency in my mind. The night that I melted on that chair opening my mind on all of them drugs, It's like my mind was opened up for a literal "spirit of anxiety" to move in and move in it did.

Eventually, all the rent and bills stopped being paid and they just got thrown into a drawer because every dime we made was going to feed our addictions. Imagine that and I hadn't even started mainlining heroin with a needle yet. We were all just sniffing it...

The party pad and our dream of having a safe place to fall safely eventually came to an abrupt end with an eviction notice slapped on our front door and my mom with her huge heart, allowed Kim and I to move in with her in the trailer park. The only problem here is that this was the home of all of these young addicted gang bangers, kids who were part of an organized crime branch in Chicago that had all gone what they call A.W.O.L. on drugs.

By this time, the trailer park had actually started to look a lot like The West Side of Chicago. The whole park was tagged with gang symbols and the selling of pounds of pot, wicky water, heroin and LSD... I had seen windshields of cars getting bricked out for trying to drive off without paying. These kids had a whole system setup for serving clients who would drive their cars in and out of "The Horseshoe."

That's what the trailer park at 88th and Archer became known as…

The Horseshoe.

Where my mom now lived was pretty much where all of our region's local drug trafficking was going on. This was not a little thing happening here. The Horseshoe became known for it's drug trafficking. There was a lot of money coming in and going out of this place and a lot of kids partying with all of it, to no end.

Let me take a moment here to say something I feel is important to point out. In all genuineness. These kids that I keep calling gang bangers actually became close friends of mine. Fellow addicts. You have to understand, that they were just kids as hurt, bound and as lost and addicted as I was. Kids with their own broken stories to tell. I often imagine our descent together to be a lot like War Vets who have fought in the same war. You just would have had to have been there to really understand the bonds that were being made between us in such horrible circumstances. We all knew we were messed up and I can remember telling everyone, as we continued to spiral ourselves further and further down and out of control, that all I knew anymore, was that our only hope was gonna have to be Jesus. I knew at this point, as our addictions got worse and worse, that truly "Only God Could Save Us."

Some would laugh and mock my only hope, others seemed to pause…

Our crowd had quickly morphed from what used to be skaters, metalheads, goth rockers and hippies with an interest in God into gang bangers, inner city dope dealers, hardened criminals and older crackheads who knew quick and easy ways to hustle a quick buck in order to keep their addictions fed. It was in no time at all that I was now smoking Crack and sniffing several bags of Heroin a day on The West Side of Chicago. Double Breasted is what they would call this in the early 90's out on the streets. All this term ever meant to me was that I now had 2 addictions to feed. I would smoke Crack to get up and then sniff Heroin to come back down.

It was an insane roller coaster that I could not get off of.

An imbalance of the chemicals that make up our brain chemistry.

I had lost the balance and was always trying to find it again with uppers and downers not knowing that the only way to find balance again was to stop all drug use and allow the lake of mind up there to settle.

I would leave Kim alone in my mom's trailer, while I would be out on the streets of the city with other neighborhood addicts learning the quickest scams and crimes to keep our addictions fed.

Instead of having a woman that I was responsible for bringing bread and butter home to, I was sick and addicted and expected to return with some weed and a dope bag. Somehow, I still had enough heart and sense about me to know that she was much safer at home than I was out there on the streets hustling for quick, illegal and ill gotten gains.

The amount of drugs I would be doing out there with my new found friends and the tolerance I was building was surpassing Kim's at an unprecedented rate. I could be sniffing anywhere between 8 and 10 bags of Heroin a day and smoking anywhere between 5 or 6 Crack Rocks all before returning home to her with 2 blows and a joint.

No, I was not a good Fiance. I was a very sick and selfish man.

It must have not been even 3 months after we got engaged that my Father in Utah got word that I was using Heroin back home in Chicago. I remember sitting in our bedroom in my mom's place nodding halfway in and out of consciousness on a phone with him when he asked "What are you on?"

I was silent... he said "Is it Heroin?" I said "Yes." He said "Tomorrow, get in the car and I will meet you halfway."

During our earlier descent in the apartment, I had tried to work a job trying to sell cars with my (still at the time living) brother Mark.

For a short stint my brother would come and pick me up for work and make us screwdrivers (Vodka and Orange Juice) and occasionally smoke a joint with me. This was great (I thought) but I could never get the hang of sales and I was often withdrawing from dope sickness at work. So one day, I told a coworker at the dealership that I could get him some good pot. I had him drive me to The West Side of Chicago. I jumped out of the car with a 20 he gave me and went into a spot I frequented, I got him 10 dollars of weed and took the other 10 for myself to buy a bag of dope. Dope sick and not wanting to wait any longer, I busted out my bag of dope in his car and sniffed it right in front of him. I asked him to not tell my brother. Well, he did tell my brother and I guess my brother then told my dad in Utah and my little secret about being on Heroin was out.

So the next morning, Kim and I were on our way back to Park City Utah for a second time.

Only this time, it wasn't for me to try and to get away from the pain and confusion of a childhood friend's murder. This time, it was to go through our first experience of what you call "The Sick." We sniffed our last couple bags of dope and we were off into the great wide open again, ready to face Heroin Withdrawal.

Do you remember when I told you earlier about my friend laying a line of Heroin out to sniff and asking me if I'd like to "Get stoned to the 10th power?"

Well, what he didn't tell me was that getting off the stuff would be like getting the flu to the 10th power. The flu to the tenth power coupled with emotional and mental insanity.

Now, I can't answer for Kim. So I don't know for sure what was going on in her mind at the time. I do know her tolerance wasn't as high as mine and so her withdrawal accounts would be more her story to tell. At 19 years old, we hadn't even been engaged a full 6 months before I was found stealing, unable to keep a job and badly addicted to Crack and Heroin.

In many ways, at this point, even with my dad being the pagan that he is, hearing his voice on the phone that evening say "I will meet you halfway" was hopeful to me.

So I left Chicago in my car with Kim that morning believing that my dad would somehow know something about how to help the both of us once we got there.

Chapter Sixteen

Solsbury Hill

I would like to say that things got better after our second trek across the country to see my dad again and actually for a little bit they did. I was 20 years old now and resolved to get out of this mess that I felt responsible for getting us both into. After all, I was the man who was supposed to be taking care of this girl but I was so out of control and she was just as lost and rebellious and broken as I was.

I'm 20 years old and after meeting my dad midway across the country in Iowa, we followed him the rest of the way back into Park City Utah. I must admit, I was completely resolved to quit for good at this time. I was very serious about getting clean, finding work in the mountains and straightening up my life, for my sake and hers. My intentions were right. My heart felt pure but our minds were still helplessly addicted to chemicals.

After a week of drying out in my dad's spare bedroom I even took Kim to Church. A girl who had bragged to me about reading The Satanic Bible and whose mom was hurt hearing her say that she no longer believed in God. In my heart and mind, I was resolved now and committed to straightening up and was ready to get a job in Utah. I thought we could start going to church, have kids together and begin a new life in another part of the country pursuing Christ together.

This was my plan.

I did find a job working 2nd shift in a pretty good company that produced airbag chambers for cars and I was moving up the ranks pretty fast. I got QS 9000 certified and was learning some N.D.T. Technology and Kim who didn't like sitting around all day at my dad's went out and found herself a job in housekeeping at a local resort. Park City is a huge tourist town and service work wasn't hard to find there in the 90's. Things were going pretty well. At least a lot better than they had been back in Chicago and I was feeling like we were on the right track. I had opened a checking account but was (wisely) giving my dad our checks to avoid the temptation that might come upon us to drink or drug them away. It was the first time we had been clean and sober ever together and I was loving it. I was praying (a lot) and fully relying on God's grace, help and strength to get us both through this trying time. We were probably clean a couple months and that's when it all started to fall apart for us again. Kim came home one day and said to me "Look what I found at work under a bed." It was a quarter ounce of pot. Sticky West Coast orange hair kind of stuff that put all the weed back home in the

Midwest to shame. The cranks in our old addicted brains started turning in the wrong direction again fast and we began conspiring immediately as to how we were going to get away somewhere and smoke this. The plan became to get some of our money from my dad and for us to go to the movies and then dip off and find a nice little secluded place to smoke weed again. He asked us if we were sure we were ready for money again and with huge reservations already having been made, knowing we were planning on getting high that weekend, we pointblank lied to him. Not uncommon for addicts.

After all, in our minds "It was just pot."

It's amazing to me how just one little lie and indulgence can be used to heap up so much guilt, shame and a sense of failure on someone that the next thing you know, a snowball effect has been put into motion that leaves you in a darkness even more dark than all the darkness you have previously known.

We drove our car down the mountain side into Salt Lake City to the movie theater and smoked that night in the parking lot. I don't recall much of anything about the movie. I believe it was Candyman (some scary movie she wanted to see). We came out with more to smoke still stashed away in the car and the next thing I knew, we were out driving around the city where the Utah Jazz played looking to score more.

Now, the system of drug trafficking was a lot different in Utah than it was in Chicago. I was used to buying all our drugs in the black community of The West and South Side of Chicago but out there in Salt Lake City it was all Mexicans selling the stuff and unlike the foil and plastic bags we were used to seeing in Chicago, in Utah they were selling everything in these little colored balloons.

I remember rolling down my window and asking a guy who looked suspect on a street corner for some pot. He replied three words that would later be the darn near death of me. "Mota, Coca, Chiva", three words that were surely going to be the end of our glorious 3 month stint of sobriety. In English this translates marijuana, cocaine and heroin. My three favorites, all in the same spot. Whether in Chicago or Utah. Be it in the African community or a Mexican one. Either in foil, bags or balloons. We had once again found our demise. Kim urged me on that evening and with the 30 dollars we had left to our name, I said "3 times… one of each."

Here's what happened. This guy snatched our 30 dollars and pushed a piece of foil and 2 different colored balloons into my hand. I handed them to Kim and began to drive.

The foil had a dime bag of pot. That was good. The blue balloon had coke in it and we thought "Alright" and the red balloon had this black, sticky, gooey looking rock like substance. Kim was really upset about this and said "What am I supposed to do with this $#%!.?" Neither one of us had ever seen anything like this before but it didn't take long for us to figure it out. I saw a tall and skinny black man a few blocks over standing on a corner just as suspect as the one we had just bought from. I pulled up and said "Hey, you get high?" He said "Yes." I said "Jump in" and he did and as I drove the car Kim showed him this black gooey rock saying "Do you know what we are supposed to do with this?"

Now I need to pause here and explain this moment in life to have probably been the poorest decision to date I may have ever made. This kind, tall and very helpful skinny black man who went by the street name "Slack" sat in the back seat of our car and navigated us to a remote, hidden place off the main streets and told me to pull over and park. He took the black gooey rock out of the foil into a spoon and said "This is Mexican Mud." "What's that?" I said. He said "Black Tar Heroin." Kim said "I can't sniff that." He then pulled out a needle and bottle cap (used for cooking heroin) and said "You don't sniff this, you shoot it." Then he said "Give me that coke." She handed it to him and like some sort of professional he began to mix them both with some bottled water and then with a lighter he cooked it and then he took a piece of cotton from a cigarette butt and with that syringe he drew up 10 milligrams and said to me "Give me your arm." Almost like I was in some sort of trance, caught up in all of the excitement and my inhibitions already down from the pot we had just smoked, I offered my arm probably as surrendered and willingly as I would imagine Christ offering his own arms to be nailed to The Cross.

He spiked me and I felt "The Rush" I had only read about and seen in movies like "The Basketball Diaries" or "Trainspotting." It was only moments later that I looked over from this new found state of bliss and noticed him doing the same to my Fiance and then, as I watched, higher than I had ever been, he cleaned up the rest of the junk in the spoon for himself.

In that state of incomparable euphoria, I already knew that I had found a place that I would never want to leave. I didn't realize that the cost to stay there though, was going to be everything good in my life...

I didn't realize that there would be no more movies or picnics in the park. No more long romantic walks or evenings out to dinner with family and friends. I didn't know that I would be giving up all the good things people enjoy in life, like a good book, beaches, pic nics, sunsets and even my Fiance.

All I knew was that at that moment, I was where I wanted to be and I knew that this pursuit to stay there might very well be the death of me. So in that moment, perhaps even prophetically, I started to pray out loud. I said "Lord Heavenly Father, please don't let this be the death of us. In Jesus name."

We were all silent in the car after that prayer. You could hear a pin drop and I was higher than I had ever been in my life. I mean, the first time I had ever shot Heroin in my arm directly into my bloodstream it was mixed with Cocaine. This is what they call "A Speed Ball." This is what killed John Belushi.

The rest of this story will be a bit more difficult to write about and it's imperative that I make clear here that I don't want any young curious minds to ever read any of this and be in any way intrigued with or impressed with any of this. It's imperative for me to make clear that the next decade of my life was a lot like living possessed by a devil, whose intention was to drag me through hell and then kill me.

I developed a horrible chemical dependency that trumped all my previous addictions and was literally being controlled and ran around by an unquenchable need for more of that mainline substance. From that evening on, after getting "Hit" by Slack (a complete stranger) all I knew anymore was to make money, get high, make more money, get high and on and on and on... For the next 7 years, with the exception of times spent in jails or rehabs, all I would know was this lifestyle of make money.... get high.... make money.... get high.

The same week we shot Heroin together, we lost our jobs up in the mountains because I was insanely put on this constant pursuit for more.... more heroin.....more cocaine.....and now more crack.

We had found some local addicts amongst the black community which made it a lot easier for me. It was more like being home in Chicago and we ended up running around learning the drug scene of Salt Lake City. I was now spending my days with local addicts, who were sleeping under bridges, staying in abandoned cars and eating at local homeless shelters.

The madness of each day thereafter would take me too much time to write in one book and honestly I could probably fill bookcases if I was to try. So it is to be with many of the events to follow, that I will choose certain select events to share with you from the next several years of my life as a Mainline Heroin and Crack addict. I mean, seriously, the unfolding of all the craziness and stories after stories, day after day, year after year, would all be impossible to tell. To even try and piece it all together in correct chronological ordering is a lot like tackling and ordering The Canon of our Holy Scriptures. I am going to be 43 years old this April 3rd and even after 19 years away from this active addiction, memories and crazy stories from the past, that I had totally forgotten about will still resurface from time to time. So I will do my best with painstaking honesty and recollection to consolidate and highlight just a few of the events that took place in Salt Lake City. Just a few stories, to give you a small glimpse into what it was like being an addict hustling that city's streets.

One scenario, I recall for example, would be me having a 12 inch butcher knife held to my throat after learning from a local hype how to sell people fake crack. Yeah, he showed me how to put drywall into little drug baggies and sell it on corners to people who would pull up in cars. I remember this angry customer and his lady friend coming back and jumping out of a car on me, this man grabbing my hair from behind and putting a butcher knife to my throat and while they were demanding their 60 dollars back, Kim who had all the money in her purse starts arguing with them, refusing to give it to them, saying this was going to be our money to eat breakfast at Denny's on.

Eventually, she reluctantly gave it back to them, he let me go and it wasn't but a few days later that we were both in agreement to pawn our engagement rings to buy more heroin...

In some sort of coherence and not wanting her to be in harm's way anymore than she already was, I went and put her in a hotel room on the mountainside in Park City, while I continued to learn more about hustling the darker streets down in The Valley of Salt Lake.

I met a man in the area who decided it would be a good idea for us both to rob some of the local drug cartel. At the time, this seemed reasonable enough to me. I had already been part of selling suitcases of ammunition to buyers in hotel rooms with this mexican guy named Arturo. I mean, I had seen whole basements under businesses filled with stolen goods like 501 jeans and TV's waiting to be resold on the black market. I was stealing cartons of cigarettes from local retailers and reselling them on the streets at markdown prices and I had already seen enough of how they were moving drugs and guns back and forth over the border between Mexico and America to know how much of this underground drug and cash system worked. So, when the idea of robbing Mexican Drug Dealers was presented to me, I thought to myself "Yeah, Why Not." By this time, I was starting to develop more and more of a hatred for dealers who were making all of this crazy money on me and my associates' addictions anyways. The song "They don't really care about us" by Michael Jackson comes to mind.

You see, in Utah in the early 90's, the pot, coke and mexican mud was being brought over the border to us straight from Mexico. These drug dealers would come into town, chop, cut and bag this stuff in a local hotel room and then give it to the street corner guys to slang (sell). This is pretty much how the system goes anywhere you go. Differing cities, same system. The ones with the weight (drugs) are rarely ever the ones on the corners selling this stuff. Many of the guys and girls on street corners you see selling drugs are actually addicts themselves selling it for a small kickback of the drug. For example; let's say for every 10 bags you sell for "The Man" you might get to keep 2 bags for your own addicted self. An easy hustle for the addict to keep their own addiction fed and hard lengthy stays in jail for the addict, while dealers are away safe somewhere counting cash.

You see, the dealers stay safe, while the addicts keep getting caught with felony possession of a controlled substance and end up doing serious time incarcerated. In the subculture of my addicted days, such individuals who were out there on the streets, selling another man's drugs, were often referred to as "Send offs." This is because they were the ones being sent off to do serious jail time while the guys distributing the weight were sitting away safe on 20 inch rims profiting on all of that cash money the servers would be bringing back to them.

So here we are, me and my new found friend "Mase" sitting in my car, at a local hotel waiting for these mexican drug traffickers to go out for breakfast so we can crowbar their door open and take all of their drugs and valuables. While going through their stuff, I found a pair of huge diamond earrings. I ran one across the bathroom mirror and almost fainted when I saw that thing cut through glass like butter. Meanwhile, Mase grabbed all the coke off the table and I grabbed a huge old school boom box that would light up when it played. On my way out, my eyes spotted these beautiful snakeskin shoes sitting by the door that just so happened to fit my feet perfectly! I ended up trading the boombox to some of their own send offs down the street for more of the coke we had just stolen from their room. All of this, while wearing those awesome looking snakeskin shoes.

So here I was with a whole lot of coke to stay high on for a while and a pair of diamond earrings big enough to retire on. It was all "good in the hood", I thought and I was feeling successful in our exploits, until some of my black friends grabbed me off the street. Pulling me aside into an alley, I was told that there was an S.O.S (which means shoot on sight) out there on me.

This was continually confirmed by many of my peers telling me that some guy named Carlos was riding around deep (with others) in a rented car and a pistol looking for the "Loco Wado" (crazy white boy) wearing snakeskin shoes.

Ooops! Yeah, I was in a bit of a pickle here.

So I headed back up the mountain side out of Salt Lake City (with Mase) into Park City to the hotel I had Kim in only to find her madder than you can imagine at me for leaving her there for 2 days with nothing but a few pieces of Kentucky Fried Chicken to eat. I threw a few ounces of Heroin and Coke on the table and began cooking us all some speed balls to shoot in our veins.

I told them both, Kim and Mase, that I seriously thought it was time for us to consider getting out of Salt Lake. For some reason, Utah just wasn't feeling very safe or welcoming to me anymore and I was all of a sudden feeling conveniently homesick for Chicago again. It was the new plan. I was just wanting to get back to Chicago alive!

I showed Kim the diamonds and she was as amazed as I was and she did the same thing with them as I did to the bathroom mirror. So collectively and as high as skyscrapers, we all decided (after shooting enough coke to kill a small farm animal) to pack up what we had and head back down the mountain, East on I 80, straight for Chi Town.

As far as I was concerned, I had sort of burned up all my options and connections that were there for me in the streets of Salt Lake City.

So high and out my mind (as was the new custom) we were doing a solid 70 mph down the mountain side out of Park City, when out of the darkness, I saw a dead moose come into my headlights and with no time to think or respond thoughtfully, I had to swerve and either clip this things head, lying toward a cliff or turn the other way toward his back and crash at 70 mph into this solid rock mountain side. So I turned left hard, clipped the dead moose's head and flipped our little ford escort completely over and upside down and slid for what the police said was a quarter of a mile on the roof of our car. Even more odd than this, was that witnesses who were driving behind us said that they saw our car headed straight off the mountain side and then watched it turn on it's roof and make it around the bend of that turn, as if something was steering it from above. What I remember, from the inside of the car was being upside down, looking at Kim, seeing a whole lot of sparks shining through the shattered windshield at our face and feeling like something was holding me firm in my midsection against my seat. I had no seat belt on and I was feeling what felt to me like a hand holding me in my abdomen area against my seat until the car came to a complete stop. Then the pressure that was holding me safe in my seat left and I fell into the roof of our now totaled car. Things moved so fast from there on. We all crawled out alive through the broken out back window. The car was completely demolished and the next thing I knew there were police and ambulance lights everywhere and I was still flying high from all the Coke and Heroin I had just shot. The people from the car behind us were telling the cops how something had kept our car on the road and Kim was sitting there nursing a cut on her knee that was going to need stitches. So here we were now alive and off in an ambulance to the hospital located back down in Salt Lake.

The city I was desperately trying to flee.

I remember sitting in the waiting room of the hospital with no car and paranoid knowing that these Mexican Drug dealers were driving around wanting to take my life. Keep in mind that Salt Lake City is a very small city compared to Chicago. Not as many places to get lost in or hide. Even the bus seemed like a crazy risk for me at this point. So I gave in and finally called my dad. He was presently dealing with cleaning up the mess I had made with that checking account I had opened when I first started working and had plans of doing well for my Fiance and I in Utah.

You see, during our descent before I was selling ammunition, retail thieving and robbing local drug traffickers, I had started writing bad checks in stores and writing them up for purchases and cash back that I didn't have any money in the bank for. In a couple of weeks time, I had written out a whole checkbook for things that I could buy and resale on the street for fast cash. My dad, God Bless him, reluctantly had to cash in bonds that he had been saving since I'd been a kid for what he had hoped would be a future college education for me. Instead, they went to the bank to make right all my debts. I guess you can say that I had chosen The School of Hard Knocks over Harvard or Yale.

He also ended up having to have our car towed and junked. My dad was working hard to clean up all the messes my poor decisions in life were leaving behind me. When all was said and done, as quickly as we had come to Park City for redemption, we were now being given two one way tickets for a Greyhound bus back to my mom's in Chicago, where I was about to learn the inner workings of a bigger city's drug trafficking scene and culture.

"What about those diamonds" you might ask?

Remember that guy Mase? When we were in the emergency room, I had left him sleeping with his head on our duffle bag while I went in with Kim to get her stitches. While I tended to her side, he decided to grab that bag and run off with those diamonds. He's probably either dead right now or perhaps somewhere in Hawaii.

By the time we made it back to Chicago in one piece to crash again in my mom's trailer, me and Kim's relationship had pretty much come to an end. Although we were still hanging on to something together, our addiction, that was sadly about it. I believe our engagement in many ways had been annulled the day we sold our rings in Salt Lake.

At this point, we were nothing more than very toxic to each other. As a matter of fact, from the very beginning, we weren't much but very toxic to each other. Our relationship was a lot like locking two alcoholics up in a fully loaded bar. We may have had our pursuit of drugs and alcohol in common but beyond that we really were not a good match for one another. To this day, I have no ill will toward her and only hope the absolute best for her and her life but let's face it, our union was no match made in Heaven.

If any regret remains in any of my recollections of our time together as addicts, it would be for any emotional wounds that she may have endured having been with a man who had not only placed a chemical dependency before her but who as well, placed it's dangling noose around his neck and right in front of her.... jumped.

For that I am truly sorry.

At home in Chicago, as I continued my pursuit of more Heroin and Crack, my life of making money to get high, while leaving her in my mom's trailer was very short lived. Our relationship didn't last any more than a year and honestly, I don't blame her at all for leaving me the way she did.

From the day we connected in my car in the parking lot of Jewel to mourn our friend's murder, to the day she walked out of my life a year later, we both had these things in common. It was music, drugs and alcohol and this was not a good foundation to build anything on. Especially a family. God forgive us. God forgive me.

From the very beginning, our relationship was a recipe for disaster. I can only pray that her and her family and friends could somehow find it in their hearts to forgive me for not manning up at that time in my life to be the man and provider I should have been.

Truth be told, I was too sick and broken and it is a grace from God that she got out and got well when she did.

My life and descent from this point on into mainline Heroin addiction in The City of Chicago had really only just begun. With Kim now gone, having moved on to get cleaned up and on a better track again with her own life, I was now on my own… again.

Only now equipped with Salt Lake City under my belt like a boot camp on how to survive the war on drugs and how to make that underground cash economy work for me in what would be the next 6 years of my life back in Chicago.

Chapter Seventeen

Heroin

Back in Chicago, in my mom's mobile home, I was an addict turning 21 years old and having already drank quite a bit. This whole turning of age thing was an occasion that really didn't mean much to me. Only Heroin and getting more of it with my trailer park friends meant anything to me. By time I had returned home from Utah, there had been some kids who were now, like myself already banging it (mainlining Heroin with a needle).

I quickly fell in with this crowd and we were allied immediately in our addictions and our pursuit of more money and dope. I almost don't know where to begin here. The few events I have shared in the previous chapter to give you a glimpse into Salt Lake City's drug scene was only a precursor to what Chicago had to offer. The Black Market of stolen goods in Chicago was a lot larger. The opportunities to make quick ill gotten gains was a lot more vast in this city and pretty much seemed limitless in the ways we could come up with quick cash.

Things got crazy. I would walk into stores, walk straight to the electronics department, grab a 400 dollar 4 head VCR (the rage of the day), rip the theft detectors off the box and then walk right back out the front door with it to jump into a getaway car.

As my tolerance progressed, one VCR could become as many as I could fit into a shopping cart. Sometimes rolling 5 or 6 of them out the front door of a store. I recall having security guards chasing me toes to heel, as I narrowly got myself and a whole shopping cart pulled into the open sliding door of my friend Ricky's van once as he smoked tires getting me and these stolen goods out of there. I mean, just to give you a picture. I have been tackled and arrested at the doors of places carrying a 36 inch (box television) on my shoulder. That was a case. I had friends of mine busted wheeling snow blowers and lawnmowers out of places. I had a friend show up by my mom's place with a Jeep door. Just the door. Asking "Where can we scrap this." Another friend of mine was busted stealing a tombstone. Can you believe that? A tombstone.

As me and my friends' arrests and addictions increased, I was easily putting away anywhere between 2 or 3 hundred dollars a day into my veins and lungs, doing some insane unlawful stuff to stay high. I remember driving around in a car with Slim, the same guy who tried to warn me about this stuff when I first got started. We were driving around in a car I had taken from another childhood friend and we saw a Trek mountain bike sitting outside of a Block

Busters movie place. I stopped the car and opened the trunk, while Slim grabbed the bike and threw it in and as we were driving off, we both saw this little kid in our rear view mirrors come running out of the store screaming and yelling for his bike. As hardened and addicted as we were... I remember us both feeling really bad about this but not in any way bad enough to go back. That bike was going to be sold in the city for dope money.

As our substance abuse grew, so did all of our creative ways to make illegal money. Instead of just walking or running out of stores with VCR's, I was given this great idea of returning stolen stuff back for cash in the same store I had just stolen it from. This made my trip to the dope spot with cash money in my hand a lot easier, quicker and safer.

Let me explain this and what I mean by safer.

For example, one day I was selling some stolen VCR's a few blocks from Cook County's Department of Corrections on 26th and California. I was on 22nd when this mexican guy came up to me and said "Hey Homes, I know you, you that Two Six." I said "No man, I ain't no two six." (two six being a street gang in Chicago that rides under the 6 pointed star.) Now I'd been selling gold, jewelry, TV's, bikes, VCRs and you name it in this heavily

"Latin King" populated area (another Chicago street gang that rides under the 5 pointed star) for a couple of years now and it was always some good quick cash for me. Until this one day. On this one particular day, while I was trying to unload some VCR's this guy comes up to me and says "Yeah, you're that Two Six" and he whistles. Not a good thing in this neck of the woods. Jay (my friend in the car) yells at me "Get in the car, Quick, Quick, get in the car!" and as I turn to look back, I see 3 guys running down the alley as fast as they can toward me and while I dodge that first guy's fist swinging at me, Jay is still screaming "Go, Go, Go" so I run and dive roll through the passenger window of this car with a VCR in my arms like Walter Payton diving into an end zone in the 80's and as we are trying to get the car out of this place, a bottle of bleach gets thrown through our back window, shattering glass everywhere and while Jay is squealing tires, trying hard to maneuver out of this small, pawn shop parking lot, these guys start kicking out the tail lights and banging on the car. Jay is screaming and scuffling hard to get us backed up and out of this enclosed parking lot before we both end up bricked, beaten or shot and to make matters even worse, this wasn't even our car. It was Jay's older brother Doughboy's car. A car we had actually stolen (or unknowingly borrowed) from his brother to ride out into the city with.

So back to my original point here, about it being safer to return stolen goods back to the same store you had just stolen them from. Deciding that this would be a safer and a better idea than selling our stolen goods in the hood. I started walking into the electronics department of some pretty prominently, well known box stores and I would grab a VCR box, sit it on the floor, break it open, rip the plastic open to make it look used and then I would pull the theft detectors off, carry it half opened back up to the customer service desk and say something like "This ate my disney movie and I'd like to return it."

Now, one of three things would always happen here. They would almost always ask me if I had a receipt. I would say "No, but I have an I.D."

Then they would either;

1.) Offer me cash back. (Win)

2.) Offer me an exchange for a new one brand new in the box. (street sale, still a win)

3.) Just tell me "No" they can't do anything without a receipt. (still got it to walk out with and sell...still winning)

So 9 out of 10 times I got cash back or a brand new VCR in the box to walk out of the store with. This same kind of thing worked on many items in many different stores. For example, carbon monoxide detectors became a favorite of mine for a while, getting me cash back at 75 dollars a piece. The only time any of the above didn't work was once a retailer had caught on to me and they had security waiting to detain me and have me arrested at the door. That would be that 1 out of 10 times that it didn't work out so well or that I would have to try and run really fast.

Whenever a new product came out on the mainstream market that was popular with the public, there was always a good value for it on the black market as well. For example, when Mach 3 Gillette Razors came out it was like hitting a gold rush for all of us "boosters" (that was the street name for retail thieves.) As a Crack and Heroin addict stealing everyday to get high, my tolerance was growing higher and higher. Now with a tolerance of about 500 dollars a day being put away into my brain and body. Stealing had become a way of life but eventually after stealing from the same store over and over again, you would inevitably get caught up and arrested and all this really meant to us, was that it was time to move on to another region and to hit up new stores.

So you would either end up getting arrested yourself in a failed attempt to boost something or word on the street would get around in the dope houses that someone else you knew got arrested there and that would be our red flag to know that the store's security was on to us. So in our lingo of the day, that meant that the store we were stealing from was now "Burnt up." Simply meaning that it was no longer a good place for any of us to steal from.

Almost needless to say, as my arrests and short stays in Chicago's Department of Corrections began to escalate so did my knowledge and insight into the world of our city's underground crime scene. Unfortunately, in the 90's, Cook County lock up to someone who wasn't ready to change their crooked ways could be a lot more like the local College for Criminals rather than a place of correction and rehabilitation. Listening to how other inmates got caught and how they could have avoided their arrest was only serving to improve and sharpen one's skills on future heists. Plus, the connections that can be made in jail while doing short stints there are nothing to be made light of. I remember drying out in Division 2 once, a place they used to call Gladiator School and being in a bunk next to this older Italian guy whose presence demanded respect even from the young, buckwild gang affiliated thugs in the facility. He was "Mob Related" and everyone knew it and unlike anyone else on our tier (no matter how gang affiliated or hooked up they were) this guy would have Cook County Guards coming onto the floor to personally deliver him cartons of cigarettes and Burger King. It was crazy The Juice this guy had. I had never seen anything like this in all of my arrests.

For whatever reasons he seemed to take a liking to me and he kept telling me that he would be out of this place in a matter of days but before he was released he offered me a job that would entail me driving a car (no questions asked) from Chicago to Mexico and from Mexico back for an easy 10,000 dollars. He told me based on the successful completion of this first job would determine how many more jobs and how much more money I could get.

It was during this same stay in County that I remember as well getting deep into The Word of God again though, for the first time since I'd been a kid jamming with my brother in his Christian Rock band.

In my younger years, I had already become somewhat familiar with The Psalms, Proverbs and The New Testament but I always wanted to know more about The Old Testament and what its implications were to the whole gospel story. So it was within this particular stay that I decided to sit up all night with my hot water and single serve packet of coffee reading The Bible from its beginning. While everyone else was sleeping, I would sit up at the end of my steel bunk with a plastic chair and my feet up reading The Bible every night.

It was honestly with Great Hunger and Thirst for Righteousness surrounded by the smell of cheap tobacco, recycled air and an all male confined living quarters that I would look forward to meeting with The Lord for these all night Bible studies together. I had such a strong desire to learn and gain a better understanding of God's Word that it became life to me in that dire place. With an open Bible and my heart continually turning to Jesus saying "Holy Spirit, Teach Me", I could feel his peace and presence in my life again and it was amazing.

I wasn't interested in driving a car to Mexico.

The only connection I wanted to make was my connection once again to Jesus. Even to this day, if I begin to wander away I can feel my soul and the quality of my life quickly begin to perish. I knew then that I had found what my heart and life would need to survive and thrive.

As a matter of fact, even though I was physically confined at this time, I had never felt better than when I was staying up all night in jail with Jesus studying The Bible during the quiet sleeping hours of everyone else.

This is also when I met John Doe. He was an extremely tall black man huge in stature. The strange thing about this guy though was that no one, not even the guards had any idea of who he really was. He had no identity. Thus the name John Doe was given to him. So here I was one night when John Doe came walking over to my bunk just as I was getting ready to sit down and study The Bible. He then quietly begins teaching me The Old Testament. Really teaching me. I mean every question I had up to this point about anything, he seemed to have clear on point answers for me and then he showed me stuff in The Bible that opened me up to deeper understanding than what I would have ever even thought possible. He explained to me the difference between the Major and Minor Prophets. He explained to me the destruction and rebuilding of the temple by Nehemiah. He fascinated me with his knowledge on Angels and all of their names and functions. It was like he took me through years of study but was somehow able to complete it and explain it all to me in one night. It was like an acceleration of knowledge and understanding being given to me and what I remember taking from that evening more than anything else, was the "Don't Forget" heeding that God had given the Israelites in Deuteronomy.

It burned in my heart for days. It was like God wanted me to know that He was going to deliver me out of that place and out of the hands of the enemy and that he was going to set me, this captive free and that he was going to make a way for me and that after he was done getting me out of this mess and done leading me out of my bondage into the land of promised milk and honey and after I had planted for myself vineyards and built for myself a home and after he had given me a wife and beautiful kids… that above all else... I must not ever forget that it was The Lord God Almighty who was going to do all of this for me.

I left our Bible study that night comforted with a deep knowing that despite my current condition and slave-like state, a slave to that addiction, I left our study knowing that God was going to prevail and get me out of all of this somehow. I didn't even have to know how. I just knew that I was going to have to believe God and trust him for it. Before our bible study was over, Mr. Doe had me write down a bunch of verses that he spoke to me from memory and when I later looked up these verses… they were all verses about angels. It was like he was some sort of walking Strong's Concordance that night in jail and by the time the sun came up that morning, we had both been through the whole Old Testament together and I had been given a greater understanding of The Bible than I ever had.

In hindsight, I do not believe the bible study that me and Mr. Doe had that night could have been naturally possible. It all had to have been supernatural and to this day, in hindsight, I believe this man may have been an angel.

It wasn't but a few days later that the guard called out my name for court. I was shipped out and returned with a "Time Considered Served" verdict and was told to pack up my stuff because it was time for me to go home. On my way out of the Gladiator School, this John Doe stopped me in the walkway and without any warning, punched me in my chest so hard that to this day even 20 years later I still sometimes feel a little discomfort and some muscular pain in that area. He hit me so hard I momentarily couldn't breath and it took all I had to not shed a tear… then in an awkward silence, he said only two words while staring me dead in my eyes... He said to me "Don't Forget."

Now let me add, although I came out of my stay there with a real zeal and passion again reignited for Jesus. My living conditions and community back at home had not changed at all and it was really no time at all until I was back running with all my other badly addicted peers again.

By time my years in this earthen hell as an addict was over I had acquired for myself over 37 arrests for criminal trespass, misdemeanor and felony theft, felony possession of a controlled substance and several violations of adult probation. I actually remember a police officer at Harrison and Kedzie (a police station I had been through numerous times) dropping a wrap sheet on me that hit the floor and rolled out about 8 feet. All of my associates were gang affiliated and I even had an F.B.I. investigation number assigned to me. I was pretty much in trouble all the time. It's sort of like I was saying in a previous chapter that there is just too much for me to possibly write about. So many stories I won't be able to disclose here. Let me say this though, although many who know me, know that I have always had to battle a pretty bad Scot-Irish temper, I was never a violent criminal. I was a thief and a Heroin addict. A kid who got hooked on Heroin during my last year of highschool and who was lying and stealing for years to come to keep my addictions fed.

At one point, I was walking into stores and walking out with 10 or more disney movies stuffed in my pants and down my sleeves. I would resell them for 10.00 each in the building projects of Chicago to single moms and their kids. I was wrong. I knew this was stealing and that stealing was wrong but to justify my unlawful actions and to somehow try and feel better about what my chemical dependency had turned me into (a thief and a liar), I liked to think of myself more as being like Robin Hood. You see, in my mind, I was just stealing from the rich to give to the poor. I mean, I figured that what I was stealing from Walmart, KMart or Target was just a small drop in the bucket for all of their annual income and that what I was getting these poor kids in the ghetto… Well, I thought that was invaluable.

Honestly, it was probably one of the only things I could find that still gave me some sense of worth and made me feel good about my hopelessly addicted and broken self. Things like this and perhaps sharing my last bag of dope with someone else who was dope sick. I guess being generous with my drugs to others around me and getting disney movies to poor kids helped me feel as if I was still somewhat of a good, caring person.

The truth be told, I have been in neighborhoods and have been around people of great material excess and wealth who wouldn't give you a dime for anything and then on the other hand, I have met people who would share their last and only sandwich with you, not even knowing where their next meal was going to come from. I wish all understood that even among the poor and downtrodden, the addicted and the thieves in this life, that there is still goodness and kindness (believe it or not) to be found. The confession and tears, the genuine brokenness and transparency, that is found in a room filled with people who have lost it all and who have nothing else to lose, can actually be quite a beautiful experience. The humility that the bottom will bring out of people who know they have a problem and who are no longer in any denial about it but who still have not yet found the tools and deliverance they so desperately need. To see a person coming into the light about their darkness is as beautiful as the sun at dawn.

So as my arrests increased, so did the slap on my hands from the judicial system, being incarcerated for 10 days, was now turning into 30 days and then 60 days and then 90 days and then 100 days and so on... Each of my stays in Cook County became increments of clean time that were helping me to see more clearly that I could actually live through "The Sick" and survive months at a time without heroin.

I remember during one of my Cook County stays I was oddly enough locked up across the hall from Randy, the young man who took my friend California Matt's life at 16 years old. To my surprise, when he heard that I was on the same deck as him, he had inmates send me a kite (message) with a fresh bag of Tops rolling papers and some tobacco. A kind of unexpected gesture from the guy who had murdered my friend. Eventually, I would run into him face to face out in the yard, when the weather warmed that year and he was looking healthier than I had ever seen him. He confided to me that afternoon as we walked around the yard that there wasn't a day in his whole incarceration (and it had been several years now) that he did not regret that night and what had happened between him and Matt.

It was also during this same stay that I got to witness a man killing another man over an argument as to whether or not the public t.v. was going to be on for Thursday Night Smackdown or The Simpsons. The one who was hit and had his head busted open, ended up bleeding out on the floor for hours before the guards ever arrived. Many times victims' families, whether the death was inflicted by the police or other inmates, would receive a letter from the state stating "Death by Blunt Trauma Wounds to the Head." When one dies like this in incarceration, sadly that may be all the family will ever really know about their loved one's death.

During another one of my stays, in between court dates and continuances, I met a young man (17 years old) who was being tried as an adult. He was gang affiliated as many in this world were and staying true to my jailhouse Bible Studies and prayer, he had sparked an interest in The Bible and wanted some prayer. By this time, my Faith was growing stronger and stronger and I could be found leading bull pin prayers of up to 20 or more inmates getting ready to go to court. Me and a couple cellmates would actually bang on steel beds and concrete walls booming and sustaining tribal like rhythms that would echo throughout the whole tier, as I would sing with all my might, songs in the evening like "We Are Standing On Holy Ground" and "I Love You Lord" never once being hushed or told to stop by anyone. I would pray for and study The Bible with anyone who wanted to and was constantly speaking scripture and sharing The Good News of Jesus with anyone who was interested. One night, me and that young man who was being tried as an adult sat down and studied the whole book of Acts together and when we were done he asked Jesus to come into his heart and to be The Living Lord of His Life.

My Mother, although she never had any money to bond me out of jail, would always show up to my court dates and beg the judge to mandate me some help. So several inpatient rehabilitation programs became another norm for me. There are a total of 5 impatient programs I had been through before I finally got clean. Four I completed and the one I did not. They all helped to educate me about my disease of addiction though. I thank God for my mom, merciful judges and my exposure to the 12 steps. They helped me take steps in the direction of Christ again, my future deliverance and freedom. The stuff I picked up along the way in and out of rehab and from recovery programs had a huge influence on my future victories in

Christ. I thank God as well for the advocate I had in my mom who like in Junior High (when they wanted to hold me back) was still showing up and going to bat for me. She was still telling people that she had faith in me and my abilities to make it. Only now, she was telling it to judges rather than principles.

Around this same time, my Mother had taken in a real nice black lady who she had worked with for sometime at Loyola Medical Center. She had fallen on some hard times herself. She was and still is a good friend to my mom even to this day. She was a very nice and encouraging lady who used to smile a lot and who asked me if I would like to go to Church with her one day. Now, when I wasn't in jail or rehab I was still medicating myself with bags of dope and smoking weed every night but I thought "Sure, why not" mostly because the church was closer to where I needed to get some more dope for that day. She took me to Bill and Veronica Winston's Living Word Church in Park Forest IL and let me tell you that Bill preached so good that day, that I threw my last 10 dollars into the offering basket and got baptized that morning in The Name of Jesus. Trust me, you know the preacher is preaching good, when a dope addict gives the church his dope money for the day.

Eventually, my dad and stepmom (to my surprise) moved back to Chicago from Utah (another job move for my dad) and after I had relapsed one evening and had died (shortly after coming out of rehab) he began paying 100 dollars a week for me to be in a local methadone program.

Wait. Let me backstep a minute here and tell you a little more about this one time that I died. I ended up suffering what they call respiratory failure and had to be injected with a substance called Narcan by paramedics to be brought back to life. Now by this time, I had already seen quite a few people stop breathing. I had administered mouth to mouth resuscitation to bring people back. I can think of at least three people on three different occasions. As a matter of fact, a friend of mine had actually broken a man's ribs once pumping his chest too hard while I was breathing the breath of life back into his lungs. We kept this man alive right up until an ambulance pulled up in the driveway. We had called 911 and informed them that he was in the basement overdosed and not breathing and once they arrived on the scene we stopped breathing and pumping and ran... I had warrants for my arrest at the time.

The next day we had heard the good news that he was alive but was at home now having to nurse some broken ribs.

I believe he would have been the third person I was able to successfully administer resuscitation. The scriptures in

Genesis that talk of God breathing The Breath of Life into Adam and him becoming a living soul is a very real thing to me. I get that. I totally get that. I have personally seen this. When a dead, lifeless body kicks back on because you have given it your breath. It's an amazing thing!

So back to the first time that I died. I was walking down these train tracks in the woods behind my mom's mobile home park with a young couple about a mile away from everyone and everything and that's all I remember. I remember walking at night with them. I had shot several bags of Heroin that day and unwisely drank a capful of what they called liquid G (a club drug) and I woke up in an ambulance with two paramedics sweating over me frantically saying over and over again "We got him, we got him." I can actually remember hearing my heart flatlined and then it beeping and me waking up.

The story goes that I fell over on the train tracks out there in those woods and this young man whose name I don't even know picked me up and carried me on his shoulder to the nearest bar he could find in Willow Springs (a neighboring town). He then laid me up against a wall in the parking lot while his girlfriend ran inside and told people that there was a man dying outside. By the time the paramedics arrived on the scene, I guess I had slid into a puddle of water and was convulsing face down in it. That evening I got to see my dad, my brother and my mom all together again at the hospital. It was the first time I had seen our whole family together since I'd been 7 years old and I just remember wanting to get out of there, away from all of them, so I could go get myself another bag of dope.

That evening, with my dad back in Chicago now, my dad intervened and made me sleep in his van with him in the driveway of my mom's trailer. I guess he was doing all he knew to do to keep me from going out that night and killing myself again. This is also when he decided to pay that hefty price of 100 dollars a week to enroll me in the 19th and Pulaski Methadone program. I was interviewed and put on 180 milligrams of Methadone. Considering the size of my habit, I was told that it was the highest dose they would give anyone.

I will never forget the 1st day I took Methadone. It was like a miracle for me. I couldn't hardly believe that I wasn't going to have to go out there and steal anymore to get high. I mean, I had been ripping and running everyday now for a good 5 straight years. You see, when you are an addict, there are no days off. There are no paid vacations. The closest thing you can get to a break is when you are staying in a rehab or you are incarcerated.

My dad also took me down to Cook County Hospital where I was diagnosed with Obsessive Compulsive Disorder, Clinical Depression and A Severe Anxiety Disorder. The one I picked up years earlier in the apartment melting my brain away on LSD listening to Pink Floyd. They diagnosed me with all of this stuff and prescribed me some really good and strong anti depressants that in time, really did seem to start helping me.

I was doing pretty well for the first time in a long time. So well that I even began taking classes with my dad at Moraine Valley for Counseling The Chemically Dependent. I mean, I honestly had not felt this free and healthy since my short stint of sobriety in Utah with my dad right before being introduced to that Ugly Mexican Mud. I was being properly medicated for depression, on Methadone and I wasn't on Heroin for the first time in years. Although I was still on chemicals (prescribed chemicals) I was ready to turn my broken heart and life back to God again and I was wanting to give a program of recovery a real, hard and honest shot. I had learned a lot from the rehab stays my mom had begged judges for and I was now going to A.A. meetings, attending school, being legally medicated and freed from the everyday obsession to use that had consumed my life for years. I mean for years, I had not been anywhere but the streets, the dope houses and the jails of Chicago. I hadn't been to a family gathering in years. I had not been out with friends to dinner or a movie. As I had said earlier, from the time I had shot dope back in Utah to the time I was free, all I had known for years was how to make money and get high.

There was this man named Al who had become my A.A. sponsor and who would pick me up everyday at my mom's trailer and take me to meetings. That man along with my faith in Christ, my mom's prayers and my dad's clinical approach, played a huge role in my future success of finally beating this monster demon of an addiction.

My life at this time, considering all the rest of it, seemed to be going great for me and I felt like I was finally headed in the right direction with God until one of my follow up appointments downtown at Cook County Hospital revealed to me that somewhere along the way out there in my addiction I had contracted an incurable disease called Hepatitis C (a chronic illness in my blood) that they told me would repeatedly attack my liver and that could very well be the death of me. A disease I was told was most likely caught from sharing needles and mixing blood with someone else out there who would have been infected. By this time, I had mixed blood with many.

In hindsight, I believe it was this news that sent me back out there again. I mean, I was doing really good for the first time in a long time and then all of a sudden, I got this news back from a routine blood draw that said I was carrying an incurable disease that could kill me.

I thought I would never be able to marry or have kids. My hope of a family one day was ruined and I felt as if there was really no reason to go on... I was angry at God. I remember weeping and yelling out loud at him from the bathtub in my mom's old place because I couldn't understand how he could have allowed something like this to happen to me.

In a way, I sort of tuned God out of my life at that time and I began to blame him for all of the repercussions and messes my own poor choices had gotten me in. I tuned Him out and began to buy into the sovereign lie that suggests all of these horrible things that had become of my life were somehow supposed to be his wonderful will and plan for me. So at this point, I honestly wasn't really wanting much to do with Him anymore. At this point, I began to medicate again with street drugs on top of all that Methadone and antidepressants. I would wake up, take my antidepressants, take a bus down to the clinic, drink 180 milligrams of Methadone, smoke a joint and then start hitting up stores again to make some fast cash to buy more crack and shoot more heroin. I really didn't feel that I had anything more to live for at this time... I can remember not wanting to live anymore. I can remember cooking up enough dope to kill myself on more than one occasion, putting it all in a syringe and then deciding to push it all into my arm only to blackout and wake up again sometime later with drool all over myself, upset that I was still breathing.

I caught more cases for possession of a controlled substance, retail theft and some more criminal trespass cases. After another 60 day stay in County, I was slowly, in increments, day by day being taken off the Methadone in Cook County Lock up and then being spit back out on the streets of Chicago where I would begin another long run at it as an addict and thief. Only now, I was feeling like a leper with this contagious virus flowing through my blood and body as well.

I was very careful from that time on to never share needles again. What I did was found a guy on The West Side (an ex heroin addict who's now a minister) who always had new needles in the package for me. His brother was a diabetic and so they always had access to new needles in the package. As a matter of fact, I can remember sitting in his house shooting Heroin one day getting ready to go to a court mandated drug drop, when a friend of mine who had just stolen a car walked in asking if anyone wanted a tattoo. He had recently come out of the penitentiary where he had honed in on his artistry skills and was now getting ready to give me a new tattoo on my chest. A tattoo of a hand pointing a pistol at you but he was so high he kept nodding out (falling asleep) while doing the work. So here I was watching the time, not knowing what I was going to do about this court mandated drug drop, knowing that a dirty drop could violate my probation and put me in jail for the remainder of my probation. So, as I was talking about it to the room, this guy I don't know from Adam and who I had never seen before says that he's been clean for over 30 days and offers me some of his clean urine. Meanwhile, the jailhouse tattoo artist wakes up just enough to pull his tattoo gun off my chest and tells me that I can use his car (the one he has just stolen). Calvin (the future minister) suggests that I keep this guy's urine hot on the heater vent in the car to meet the temp standard on the court's mandated test tube. So here I was a few minutes later, with this guy's urine in a baby food jar, held to the heating vent, in a stolen car, pulling up into the parking garage of Cook County Corrections Center, to take my probation officers court mandated drug drop.

Anyways, I made my way through the drop and back to that place to finish my tattoo. Later that week, in that same

West Side apartment my good friend Paul (Skater Paul) , the one who gave me my first line of dope and showed me what it was like to be stoned to the 10th power, shows up, overdoses and dies right in front of me. He stopped breathing, turned whiter than a sheet and his lips went dark blue. Everyone in the house was frantic and freaking out as Smooth and Calvin screamed and kept dumping buckets of ice water on top of him. They were slapping him repeatedly really hard and yelling "Wake up Paul, Wake up!" I remember after all else had failed, falling to my knees and for the first time in a while, I reconciled to the God of my youth and I cried out saying loud enough for them all to hear… "In The Name of Jesus, Paul, I command you to get up" and he did. To my own and everyone else in the room's surprise, he opened his eyes, took a deep breath and returned to us here in the land of the living where he still remains with us to this day. He remains with us alive and the last I heard was actually doing very well in life. Thank You Jesus.

After several years of stories like this and with more days than I could ever write about, I was just about to finish doing my two back to back terms of felony probation at 2 and 1/2 years each. Which means I was almost through with completing a total of 5 years on felony probation, when I had violated my probation again for the 3rd time.

Chapter Eighteen

I Fought The Law

Let me tell you about this saint of a woman named Judy, my Cook County Mental Health Probation Officer. She was a small in stature woman, who was not scared to put me in my place. She was a short, tough lady, who would chain smoke cigarettes like a factory smokestack. She cussed like a sailor and would scream the truth about me in my face. One day, while I was sitting in her office at 26th and California. She had got to yelling at me real good but it was more like she was yelling through to me. It was more like she was yelling through the fog of depression, anxiety and addiction that I was in. I was so messed up and burnt out. At this point, Ozzy Osbourne was looking like Albert Einstein next to me. I had even overheard them talking in the cubicle next to me about me being so fried that they were considering putting me in a nursing home. My depression was so bad at this time that I couldn't even hold eye contact with anyone anymore and I could hardly lift my head up to connect with anyone in front of me and when I did find the strength to lift my head, it would only be for mere seconds before my head would droop back down with my eyes fixed safely back on the floor in front of me. In fact, the only time I wasn't in this darn near catatonic state of lethargic stupor was when I was shooting dope or smoking crack. I was such a broken mess.

It's almost as if without drugs, I had become nothing. I was constantly either in this state of hyper, dangerous intoxication or withdrawing, filled with these feelings of deep worthlessness, fear, anxiety, depression and despair, trapped in this paralyzed state of disassociated slumber.

It was truly like being dead.

It was like being dead as the bible says, in all of my transgressions.

"because of His great love for us, God, who is rich in mercy, made us alive with Christ even when we were dead in transgressions"
~ Ephesians 2:4-5

Al (My A.A. sponsor) would still come and get me at my mom's trailer for meetings whenever I was making another honest attempt at it but if I was intoxicated that day in any way, all he would say is "Call me when you're sober."

I was right in the middle of the fight of my life. My mom saw that I was struggling hard to make it but it was just way too hard for me to stay clean in that trailer court. Friends would come by while she was at work and I would be off with them again and again to the races. My mom was at her wit's end with me. There were days when my hands were swollen up like half sized softballs. I used to have to cut holes in the bottom of my sleeves and slide my thumbs through them to keep my punctured swollen hands from being seen in public and after the veins in my arms had collapsed, I had to start shooting in my feet.

I remember these 2 younger heroin addicts from the neighborhood. I was about 23 and they were only 18 and 19. This kid and his friend would pull up in this real nice blue pimped out kind of a ride with crazy rims. Him and his friend started showing up to my mom's place everyday wanting me to steal "Disney Movies" to get us all high for the day. So one day, the friend (who had just done a little time in Cook County) supposedly had made this great connection for dope in jail. So all of us, with a pocket full of cash and this kids beautiful ride, pulled up to some unknown dope spot, I had never been to in Englewood Chicago. Now do you remember Jay? The guy who had stolen his brother's car and got me out of being shot on 22nd street. Well, me and him and his older brother doughboy (Brian) were all in the backseat of this kids car, when Jay decides he would be the one to jump out of the car and cop our dope for the day. So Jay jumps out of the car and runs down the alley. He dips off out of sight and after we were sitting there waiting a couple minutes, these 2 black guys with pistols climb into the front seat of the car and start demanding all of our money, shoes and pagers from us. I was wearing combat boots and had no pager and Jay who was in the alley had all of my money on him, so fortunately they didn't get anything from me. Doughboy (Jay's older brother Brian) while taking off his Nike's, starts saying over and over again to these 2 guys with pistols in our face "Where's my brother? Where's my brother?" One of the guys points his gun in Doughboy's face and says "Oh that dude, we shot him." Now understandably so, Brian starts crying and he's saying "No, no, no" and that's when I looked at him and said "Brian, do you see any silencers on these guns?" Then I looked at this guy with his gun in my face square in his eyes and in that moment being more concerned about consoling my friend than valuing my life, I said "If you had shot him I would have heard it." There was a long silence in the car, that seemed a lot like forever, as this guy stared at me silently and very seriously back in my eyes and then with a big sudden smile on his face, he began to laugh and told us all to get out of the car. They drove off that day with Jimmy's car leaving us poor suburban white boys standing there broke, stranded and shoeless in the middle of Englewood... Well, they were shoeless.

That's when we heard Jay shout "Hey" and we saw him come running out of an alley about a block away. So here we were without a car, with no money, all of them shoeless and worst of all, dopeless. All of us are still alive though. This kid's parents made a police report on the stolen vehicle and I guess a week later, they caught one of the guys in a line up still wearing their son's shoes.

My mom, not knowing much about what was going on, except that I was dying, and in danger alot and always getting arrested, made the bold decision to sell her trailer for much less than she had bought it for, just to get me out of that place. She made a lot of sacrifices to try and help me but to me it just felt like I was the reason my mom had lost 2 homes now. We ended up moving a couple of towns over into an apartment in Burbank IL. Another small suburb just a few minutes outside of Chicago.

By this time, I was facing another arrest, violation and conviction. So here I was in Cook County again being sentenced to 4 and ½ months in another rehabilitation program called H.R.D.I.. It was held in division 8 of Cook County's lock up and it was sort of like being in boot camp. It was similar to the other rehabs I had been in, except it was while incarcerated at 26th and California in the Department of Corrections. It was always 7:00am feet on the floor kind of stuff. We had to shout mantras in unison like soldiers, yelling things like "I will be a good law abiding citizen. I will not use illegal substances. I will not steal from my fellow man" and so on… It was good stuff.

I remember Judy, the probation officer who really seemed to care about me showing up behind bars my first week there to tell me that this was going to be my last chance. Now this lady had gone way out of her way to help me in the past. I had done a lot of time on paper with her. Almost finished 5 years before I caught my 3rd V.O.P. (Violation of Probation). So here I was in this program they had going on in division 8. My stay here was a lot more effective than several of my other stays just sitting around in General Population. I was actually told that there was an 80% no return rate of repeat offenders after completing this program, an in house jail program that educated inmates on their disease of addiction. It was militant like, very educational and an overall, very good program. A huge shout out to Harold Jr. who over saw this program and who to me is still an unsung Chicago Hero.

It was also here in this program, that I had another strange late night encounter with an angelic inmate worth mentioning. I was staying true as I always did, when incarcerated, to my late night bible studies with Jesus. During this particular stay, I was in dorms rather than cells and would have to yell from my room down the hallway and get the guards approval to go to the washroom down by the mess hall. I would come rolling out of my room and the guard would not only let me go down to the washroom but afterwards, I would dip off into the mess hall where there was just enough light from a street light coming in through a caged window for me to see the pages on my Bible. I could sit there for hours reading and it never seemed to bother him. This same guard used to whoop me during the day at chess as well. Although, I did finally beat him once before my release date.

So here I was, as usual in the quietness of the night, away from the loud commotions and dramas of the day, reading The Bible with Jesus while everyone else slept, when a young man who looked to be no older than 21 comes walking into the mess hall and introduces himself to me as David. He was really cool and nice but I remember thinking to myself how out of place he seemed there. He was white with his hair slicked back like a greaser from the 50's. The bottom of his jail pants were rolled like James Dean and he wore a plain white T-shirt with a pack of cigarettes rolled up under his sleeve on top of his shoulder. He told me he was Jewish and after asking me what I was reading about, he taught me a whole bunch of stuff about Jewish History that I had not known. He started with the migration of The Jews after World War 2 back to Israel.

He explained to me about the Jewish and Arab conflict of 1948. He told me in detail about the 6 day war of 1967. He told me stories about how him and his friends used to drink at the foot of Mt. Sinai and how at sunset you could hear what sounded like voices and whispers coming off the wind of the mountain. He said that there were always Jewish soldiers who would guard the mountain and that people weren't allowed on her. He explained to me how much of a melting pot Israel had actually become and how he wished more people realized that. He told me that it wasn't like everyone who was within Israel's borders were all good, God fearing Jews who worshipped The God of Abraham either. He said that there were people of all differing religions and backgrounds... Some Christian, Some Jews, Some Muslim.... He said it was a lot more like it actually is here in The United States. He said that it amazed him, how so many people actually believed somehow that just because you were within that border that it somehow meant that your life was more precious or valued by God than others who lived or remained outside of it. He gave me an amazing insight and history of The Jewish People that I had not yet known.

It was some 18 years later and after confirming over and over again in personal study all the facts that this young David had shared with me in our late night meeting that night, I was vacuuming a floor one day at work, when his pleasant smile came to my mind and I heard The Holy Spirit clearly say to me...

"Do you ever remember seeing him during the day?"

Goosebumps radiated up and down my arms for like a minute straight and I realized in a moment of clarity, that it would have been impossible for this young man no older than 21 to have shared with me in detail, facts about his fighting in the 6 day war of 1967.

I guess I was too strung out at the time to realize it but after a couple decades of healing, it later came clear to me, in that moment, that I was asked that question.

This must have been another late night Bible Study Angel, giving me more integral pieces that have become my present day theology.

Remember me telling you about Judy, my probation officer who put me in there. She was a real Earth Angel as well. Not a real angel like Mr. John Doe or David but an Earth Angel who had been really good to me. She even bought me an acoustic guitar and brought it to me in my mom's new apartment in Burbank and then helped me take the steps I needed to get my G.E.D..

You know what? I amazingly passed that test and in doing so was told that I had scored in the top 7% of the country for interpreting and understanding the literature arts. I was even told that St. Xavier College was willing to offer me a scholarship to their school if I was able to maintain a B grade point average. Judy used to tell me ,"Scott, your friends are losers. They are all like piranhas eating each other alive but you are different. You aren't like the rest of them." She really encouraged me and made me start to believe in myself again but when I pawned the guitar she gave me to get high, I think it upset her.

You see, even though I had made some good strides in the right direction, I just couldn't seem to keep it together and keep it together for very long. I would relapse and go on these long binges of use and at the end of these runs I would often show up back up at my mom's place to crash, shower, eat and then run again. This was until my probation officer advised my mom to get a restraining order issued against me. She also started telling my mom that if she kept opening the door to me that she could have her arrested and charged for aiding and bidding a criminal.

Yes, I had made some huge positive strides in the right direction and being at my mom's new place in Burbank I was closer to local A.A. meetings. I was right where I needed to be. I just needed to stop relapsing. I was a chronic relapser who would keep getting back up and going for it but it was on these relapses that I would as well keep getting myself back in more trouble with the law.

One of the gold mine discoveries for many of us addicted young men and women looking for better ways to support our expensive habits in those days was what we called "chinging." You could take a car antenna, bend the tip into a small "L" shape, file the top down flat and use it to pull the quarters out of the change drop of a pop machine. You could easily get 10 to 30 dollars out of each machine you chinged. So if you could imagine us starting on the top floor of these hotels in Chicago and working our way down places that had 20 floors or more. Well, that was just a lot of change to cash in and equalled us getting really dangerously high everyday.

Here's how it would work. One guy would stand in the hallway outside of the ice machine room while another would start pulling quarters. If anyone came out of the elevator or their room your lookout would simply say "Hey, can you get me a Coke?" and your guy "chinging" would know to stop, get up off of the floor and buy a coke. One of my most memorable moments of "chinging" would have been at The Palmer House Hotel during one of President Bill Clinton's visits to Chicago. There was the whole fleet of black cars, people flashing cameras and secret service was everywhere while we worked our way down the whole place. If I remember correctly, we made it out of there with over 300 dollars in quarters that evening. Then we went down the street and hit a couple more hotels. It was an insane amount of drugs and money we were doing and spending those days.

With my last arrest for theft ever... I had an amazing grace meet me in jail. I'd just plead guilty to the P.D. (Public Defender) and he said with my criminal record that I was going to be doing at least 3 years minimum in prison. I had already been in Cook County Corrections Center for some time and I was hoping to get another "time considered served" and be put back out on the streets to hustle again.

Fortunately though, I had finally burnt up all those graces with the judicial system and as I stood there in custody at 26th and California that day, I remember looking through a little window from my bull pin and seeing my arresting officer sitting there in court ready to testify against me. Really scared about having to do 3 years behind bars, I began to squeeze a little pocket size N.I.V. Bible I had in my back pocket. It's a tiny little Bible I had been reading in jail and I had made a vow to God that morning to never steal again if he would get me out of this one. This is how that life changing morning went down. The guard opened the cell door. Called my name and walked me out in my cuffs and D.O.C. outfit (as is the norm when you are in state custody). I walked up to the podium with my P.D. (as I had many other times before) and as soon as the D.A. (District Attorney) started to speak, the judge said "Is the arresting officer in Court?", the D.A. said "Yes, your honor" and the Judge said "Where?" The room was silent while there were about 30 more men behind me awaiting their own convictions and acquittals that day. The D.A. sort of frantically looked around the room and said "I'm not sure, your honor" and the judge then picked up his gavel and said "Case Dismissed."

Well, he might as well have said "Amazing Grace" and dropped that hammer down because to me that is exactly what I had felt and heard that day and I did not take that miracle lightly. It has been 20 years to the day since I have stolen anything from anyone. I was always told that if you make a promise to God, you keep it.

I would rather not make promises to anyone than to make one and break it. Especially God.

The problem that prevailed though, was that I was still an addict. So even though I had acquired a good healthy fear of The Law knowing that I would be going down for a while if I was to ever get busted stealing again. I instead began walking around the streets of my neighborhood panhandling each day to stay high. I became that guy who would walk up to you on the street and say "Excuse me sir, could you spare a dollar?" or "My car just ran out of gas and I was wondering if you had anything you could help me out with?" I didn't even have a car or a license anymore. My car had been stolen and my license had been revoked for years. That's a whole other story.

So I guess the conviction I had received from The Lord on stealing that day in court was great for limiting my criminal activities but The Lord's conviction had not yet made its way into my lying and newfound panhandling ways.

It's unbelievable how much I walked over the next year being a panhandling addict. It really slowed my using down. At one point, my mom said that she thought they might have to amputate my feet. I would get up early in the morning, strap shoes on my feet and panhandle up my first 15 dollars of the day to catch a bus down to the spot and get my first bag of dope for the day.

Many days, I would leave out as early as 5:00 am in the morning on the bus and I would be out there on The West Side well past the time the buses would be running, so I would have to walk home from wherever the day and my addictions had left me. It was quite normal for me to be walking from the city somewhere like Cook County Hospital (good hustling spot) to my mom's apartment all the way back in Burbank. That's a 13 mile walk.

I can go on and on about different kinds of schemes and scams as they are called (ways to get quick, illegal and ill gotten gains) but I feel no need. What I would rather focus on now is how crucial and pivotal this promise was that I had made to God that day in court to not steal anymore. I was now actually having to work much harder for my money each day and the result played a huge part in weaning me off large amounts of dope and wearing me down to this place of just barely getting by and truly being tired of being sick and tired all of the time.

All of the walking and begging had a huge impact on my momentum and daily use, where at the height of my addictions a year earlier I could be using easily 2 or 3 hundred or even at my height 500 dollars a day, I was now down to 20 or 30 dollars a day, like when I had first began using. This was a huge difference and one step closer to my end with all those drugs. All because I made a promise to God not to steal anymore and had decided to stick to it.

All of this, the arrests, the rehabs, A.A., the deaths and even my week long stay in Madden Mental Institution for being suicidal was all becoming a real tipping point for me here in my life. I was still addicted and out there pretty bad though... I smelled. I wore the same clothes for weeks and I had caught yet again another case, not for theft but this time for another felony possession of a controlled substance. So at this point, per the advice of my probation officer, my mom decided to get that restraining order and to not unlock her door to me anymore and as hard as this was for her to do, I can honestly say that this "Tough Love" was really the best thing she could have ever done for me. Especially at this point in the game. It was pretty sad and what many would call pretty pathetic for me at this point in life and sometimes I would end up back over there in her apartment building curled up in the corner of the building's laundry room. I remember finding an empty storage bin with no lock in another building down the street that had nothing but a milk crate in it that I could sit on and sleep leaning up against the wall. I recall curling up on heating vents that winter outside of Mt. Sinai Hospital at Ogden and California and even faking an ankle injury that year so I could get out of the cold at Cook County Hospital.

At this point in the story, I would like to focus on the pain, brokenness, despair and what kinds of poverty I had seen amongst the sickest most addicted lifestyles in this City. I have seen everything from 10 kids all sleeping and huddled under blankets in a bed in a house with no heat in the middle of a Chicago winter to people having to borrow buckets of water in the summer from neighbors to drink and wash up with. I have slept in dope houses and abandoned buildings and throughout the years, I'd become friends with many of the citys hopelessly addicted and homeless. I used to sell my blood to U.I.C. for an ongoing Hepatitis C research program at the intersection of Cicero and Madison for clean needles and 30 dollars a pop. I have sold pairs of socks (2 for 5) on these West Side streets intersections throughout the mid 90's just to keep my Heroin addiction fed. I have sold bootleg movies in the city with fellow addicts and even drawn water for my needles from the lake in Douglas Park. I was in the thick of it as a young white, addicted to Heroin, street kid, getting older and older, growing sicker and sicker and on the brink of death more than once, when I found myself living and doing life with the sickest of the sick in this city.

There was a subculture of the sickest of the sickest addicts at the bottom of this great city of Chicago and that pond was what I waded in for many years.

I don't want to sound boastful but by the time I was done out there I had gained a bit of a name for myself. For example, if a new dope spot was opening up on The West Side of Chicago and there were 20 people standing around waiting for their first distribution, it was common for me to be brought up to the front of the line and served first. I guess as a once valued, now pitied customer.

There was also that growing danger of fatal relapse for me at this time as well. After weaning down to such a low dose a day, overdose can become accidental because when you are an on and off again addict with these kinds of street drugs, the chances of fatally overdosing become much higher for you than when you are a good, steady everyday user. I have had many friends die this way. It's rare that I have heard of someone dying while in their active addiction. It's usually the story that so and so was clean and doing well for a while and then they relapsed and were found dead on their bedroom floor, behind the bathroom door or even on the side of the road somewhere.

One night, It was cold. So cold. Very cold, during a Chicago winter and my feet were feeling wet, frozen and burning. The buses had stopped running to the Orange line and I was too cold to walk anywhere anymore. I know it had to have been after 10:00 pm some time and I was utterly defeated, broken, exhausted and spent. I remember lying my back up against a wall in an alley with my head tucked into my hood as far as I could get it, to keep the frigid air off my face and I was nodding in and out of consciousness. This is when another strange supernatural sort of phenomenon took place in my life. This girl appeared to me in the alley out of nowhere and asked me if I wanted to go to church with her. Now, I remember it being in the middle of the night and thinking to myself "Where are we going to be going to church at this time?" Then to my amazement, we were both standing at the corner boarding a bus and I ended up at Bill and Veronica Winston's Living Word Christian Center In Park Forest IL...

Now I had been there before, as I had mentioned previously with my mom's friend but this was not a usual service. It was a much smaller crowd than what I was used to seeing there and there was a lot of praying in tongues, casting out of devils and deliverance ministry going on. The girl who brought me there actually fell down in the prayer line next to me and puked on herself after being prayed for. They prayed for me as well and when we left, I never saw this young lady again. I had often wondered, if I would have died out there that cold winter night if it wasn't for this strange, middle of the night, church invite and what was even stranger is how sober and clean and clear I felt afterwards and how the clock said that it was now only 8:00 pm in the evening. The CTA buses were running again as usual. Go figure...

None of it makes any sensible sense to me even to this day but it all did in fact create a great deal of new and restored faith in me.

The song Rescue by Lauren Daigle comes to mind.

It wasn't many months after this in the springtime that I found myself once again cooking up enough dope to kill myself and shooting it all into my arm in an alley under an abandoned building's stairwell across the street from Ogden Courts. A housing complex that has been torn down but that was known for massive amounts of drug trafficking back in the 90's. I quietly made my way down a small basement staircase in an alley hidden away from everyone and on that last step I shot enough dope to die that day and knew it as I did it. I was done and just didn't care anymore but I woke up across the street lying on my back on a park bench in the rain at Douglas Park looking up at a beautiful smiling black woman who had told me "You fell out son but don't worry, you're going to be all right now."

I felt the cold rain hitting my face and saw the sun behind her and felt almost as if with those words "Don't worry, you are going to be alright now" she had spoken prophetically to my life. "You're going to be alright now."

As she walked away, I thought to myself over and over again, after almost a whole decade of being in that region of the city, I had never seen her before, nor had I ever seen her again and as she walked away into the rain that day, I experienced a fresh new wind of change and strength come into me. It was almost as if this angel of a woman had breathed more than just her breath into me that morning.

To sum up this chapter in my life and book and to move on now to some brighter days of deliverance and freedom, let me just say that I was pretty much shipwrecked and left for dead at this point and that no matter how far gone or how far out there and lost you maybe, let me tell you that I have been to the bottom of some places and even there, there was still hope to be found. No matter how torn up you were or even are and no matter how lost or bound you may be in anything at all... There is still HOPE as the rest of my story will hopefully show you from here on out...

With God ALL things truly are possible.

Chapter Nineteen

A Change Is Gonna Come

I was doing a stay in my last rehab ever. It was 28 days in Chicago's Downtown Haymarket Facility. It was 9-11, the day the twin towers were attacked. I remember us all being in this place right next to the Sears Tower in Chicago wondering if we were going to be hit by planes as well. Chicago had become like a ghost town and it was very odd for something to still our whole city the way those planes did on that unfortunate day.

On a single day pass, that I was granted by the rehab a week later, I had made myself down to Lake Michigan where I successfully stayed clean and spent the whole day with The Lord on the lakefront thinking about all I had come through and thanking him for my new found life and sobriety. Something was different this time. I wasn't white knuckling it. I was actually, for the first time ever, feeling a deep sense of gratitude. Grateful to be alive and not having to rip and run and lie and steal anymore to feed my relentless addiction.

The miracle had happened and the obsession to use had left me. I was actually happy to be clean and sober again for the first time in what seemed like a really long time. As I sat there alone with Jesus on the beach that day taking in the sun, the water, the sky and sand, I watched a man and his child off in the distance playing on the lakeshore together. The man, I'm guessing would have been in his 30's or so and the little boy couldn't have been more than 3 or 4 years old and as I watched this man pick this laughing little child up and swing him over his head, it was in that life changing majestic moment of long awaited clarity that I knew more than anything else ever, that I deeply wanted to know the love of a good woman and one day be a Father.

I deeply wanted to know the love of a healthy home and family.

I was also painfully aware of how much more work needed to be done on me before I would ever be ready for anything like that. So I'd begun praying that day for my future wife 3 years before I had ever even met her. I continued my pursuit of sobriety from that day on with A New Hope, Reason and Why.

Now, I know that this may sound crazy. After all I have just shared with you about my life up until this point but this day was like the dawning of a new day for me. A bright light of new realization, a purpose and new meaning being birthed in me and from that day on I actually did have something to fight and live for. It would be for the wife and children I had not yet met or even had.

My hope of having and regaining the home and family life I had lost as a child somehow outweighed the evil forces that were always trying to draw me back into addiction and death. Whenever I would start to think about getting high again, I would first immediately imagine breaking a syringe violently in half between my two fists and then I would secondly revisit this image in my mind of that man swinging his little boy around on the beach that day.

In hindsight, it all makes perfectly good sense to me now. All of those years of abuse and addiction was me self medicating all of the hurt, pain and wounds of abandonment, neglect, instability and confusion that my own dysfunctional childhood experiences left me wounded and afraid with. I was trying to numb out with large amounts of drugs and alcohol all of the shattered reflections and painful memories of my own troubled past along with all the new shame and guilt that had accumulated inside me over the years as an addict. So on that day, sitting there on the beach, it was like God began giving me hope that became like a heavenly hyssop on all of my old battle scars.

It was like God gave me an epiphany that I was going to be The Father I felt I had lost and that I was going to have the family and healthy home that I had always wanted to have.

I had a couple brief relationships with some girls after this moment of clarity but it seems that my new straightforward approach toward the women may have been a bit too much for them. I mean, here I was a clean and sober man for the first time in a decade, wanting to get married and have children and not being much qualified for any of that. I mean, I hadn't been able to hold down a steady job for years and my chronic relapsing made me a man that any woman in their right mind would not have put any bet or money on.

I mean, I wasn't skilled in any trades and my documented education was very limited.

My honest earning ability wasn't much more than a high school drop out and my street manners and lifestyle were still pretty blaring and quite evident. I talked like a white kid who just spent a decade on The West Side of Chicago. I joke today and say that the only thing I had going for me was that I was fluent in two languages.

English and Ebonics.

After running as wild as I did for so many years answering and submitting to no one, it honestly wasn't very easy for me but learning to submit and how to listen was what I finally had to learn to do. I realized that I would have to conform a bit to the conformity I had always deep down (and even still sometimes) despised. I never liked the idea of conforming to a world that was built on principles I at times deeply and internally disagree with. I never really wanted to be like and do like everyone else does. As a young metalhead, goth, hippie, punk rocker I was very anti establishment and even to this day, if I discern that the motives behind an establishment are for profit over people, I will have issues with that establishment be it political, religious, medical, educational and so on…

I believe in many ways, I was too profoundly impacted with the transcendentalist writers and literature of the 19th century to be put on that march for materialism and excessive financial wealth.

For me, at that time in my life (early on in sobriety) it had all become more about finding that continual replenishing well of peace and contentment in Christ on the inside, that I could draw life from, rather than the endless pursuit of these fleeting fixes and external substances that the drugs and money had to offer me and that at the end of each day only left me lacking and wanting more of... Concerning the money and drugs, those were things I was now having to let go of... in order to stay clean...to stay clean on the inside.

Many of Thoreau's writings such as;

> *"A man is rich in proportion*
> *to the number of things he*
> *can afford to let alone."*

And The Prophet Isaiah's words that helped me when he asked;

> *"Why spend money on what is not bread,*
> *and your labor on*
> *what does not satisfy?"*
> *~ Isaiah 55:2*

Or Emerson who once said;

> *"Once you make a decision,*
> *the universe conspires to make it happen."*

From that day on the beach, I had made the decision to go with Jesus and surrender myself to a New Life in Christ that I knew God was offering me and these kinds of readings, questions, answers and decisions that had deeply impacted my logic and way of thinking became principles I was now going to apply and practice. At this time of renewal and after years of having spent more money on drugs than many will in a lifetime on necessities, I was now experiencing serenity and gratitude for still being alive and learning to be thankful even if it was only for my mere basics on Earth like breath, food, water, health, clothing and shelter.

I was learning now after a decade of self medicating with these dangerously addictive indulgences to look up from my broken and bankrupt slumber to thank God for all the little things that I could see others taking for granted. Things like access to clean drinking water, my meals in a day, the clothing on my back, a roof over my head and the people in my life who still genuinely loved and cared about me...

I was starting to realize that regardless of what money was in the bank, I didn't even have a bank account, I was starting to realize how much wealth there was to be found in the little things that are actually the huge things that are so worthy of our continual unceasing gratitude and praise.

An awareness of all that I actually still had, began to wash over any old feelings of any lack or want I may have previously had. I mean, the obsession to use had lifted like a demon taking flight off of my back and I had begun to taste and see again just how good The Lord really had been to me. How merciful, patient, long suffering and kind he had been. The skies began to look brighter to me at this point and the grass everywhere greener. I even started to pick up people's trash and litter around local businesses because I was starting to see how beautiful Earth was and how neglected and abused she was by multitudes who had yet had their eyes opened to her beauty. I began to feel a deeper connection to our planet and a realization of my own body being fashioned and formed by God from her same clay. I developed a deep appreciation for all that had been given to us in her and started to see how much work and love that Our Father must have put into this great big ball of water and dirt for us all to live and work and play and thrive on. The sun became more real to me as our source of light and the rain, a saving grace being offered to us all regardless of origin, religion or creed. I became connected and aware of the majesty of the sky, the earth and the sea and everything in between and the wind being all of our shared breath.

I could see that everything that moves and has life, whether that be the trees, the birds or each other, it was all alive and moving because of this same common breath we breathe and I realized that The Spirit Wind of God was a grace being given to us all. Whether we were right or wrong, good or bad, righteous or wicked.

King David's words in the Psalms became alive to me and I could see it and I could hear it in the songs of the birds each morning exactly what he meant when he said;

"Let everything that has breath praise The Lord."

~ Psalms 150:6

Having been freed from the obsession to "make money and get high" was truly a miracle for me. To be able to lift my eyes off the ground I had been staring at for years and to actually see and even notice the sky again. To feel the Earth beneath my bare feet and to notice the wind on my skin and in my lungs. To hear the birds singing God's praises every morning. To notice the climate change and seasons and to re-experience the beauty of God's creation in so many new ways. I can remember laughing again for the first time in a long time, a real, non-drug induced belly laugh, for the first time in a decade.

It was all nothing short of a miracle! I was free to actually go out to the movies and dinner again and take walks around a large lake or park and not be trying to figure out in my addicted mind where and when I was going to get my next drug or drink.

I was free at last on the outside but still locked up a bit with some remaining hurt, pain and unforgiveness on the inside. It was something about seeing that man with his boy on the beach that day that not only gave me a future and a hope to live for but it also reminded me of all the pain, bitterness and unforgiveness I was still holding onto inside, for my parents past mistakes.

I had one more stay in Cook County lock up I was going to have to get behind me to settle all my dues and debts to the courts and the most pivotal point in all of my recovery and deliverance from those years of active addiction was during my last stay there when one night I was pondering deep Matthew Chapter 6.

Jesus said *"If you can't forgive others their own trepasses against you then God in heaven won't have to forgive you your own."*

It was in those words to me that I realized how deeply I needed to forgive both my Mother and Father for their inability to have worked it out and provided for me and my brother a happy home. It was in those Red Letter words that I realized I had to find it in my heart to forgive them both, for any of the mistakes I felt they had made in my childhood.

I realized that I had to forgive them, for not working it out and divorcing, that I had to forgive my dad for leaving us and that I had to forgive my mom for any abuse I felt I had endured during all of her mental and emotional breakdowns.

Here I was finding myself at the end of what had been a very long, hard and tiresome road… yielded and still… hearing from God in a jail cell, with an Open Bible, knowing that I only had to truly forgive.

Up until this point, being a grown man in great need of much forgiveness and healing myself, I was a man still holding on to the painful memories I had endured as a child and it was there in that "moment" that I realized that it was finally time for me to put these childish things away and I knew that it would not fully come, the forgiveness I needed, until I was willing to forgive.

I needed to Forgive who I felt had hurt and trespassed against me.

"Our Father" and "Forgive Us" I had now realized and experienced in a deep, refreshing and freeing new way.

It was as if the realization of my own failures and my own need for forgiveness would be completely contingent upon my own willingness and ability to forgive others... theirs.

"If you forgive anyone's sins, their sins are forgiven; if you do not forgive them, they are not forgiven." ~ John 20:23

To this day, I believe that even the ability I was given to be able to forgive them was a grace given to me at that time by God who heard my wounded heart all locked up in a jail cell, crying into my pillow again like when I was a child desperately needing God's deliverance and healing. I cried out to him and he heard.

So with an open Bible, the positioning and timing was perfect for me to see and receive the warmth and light of God's Amazing Forgiveness being lavished on me like one basking in The Glory of The Sun. The Holy Spirit began a very real and tangible transformation in my life that day. The day I was willing to forgive those that I had been blaming for myself.

I was locked up on the outside, still incarcerated but the second I forgave...

I experienced great freedom on the inside.

Just like the day I got baptized as a child.

It's like I was born again.

Clean on the inside.

When I forgave mom and dad, I felt the very same forgiveness I was deeply longing for, like this was something I had to give, to get.

A healing came into that cell that evening that was real and measurable. Not just words repeated after someone else but a real softening of the stone walls I had placed around my guarded and frightened heart for many, many years.

I Let Love In.

"Above all, love each other deeply, because love covers over a multitude of sins."
~ 1st Peter 4:8

I guess it was what one might call the beginning of true repentance. The day I forgave them the wrongs they had done me, my thinking was shifted and my logic cleared and I was given a new lens in which I could see everything and everyone more compassionately through.

I could see how we all need forgiveness.

All of a sudden, everyone was justified, loved and forgiven.

Even the hardened criminals I was locked up with.

I had been so blind but now for the first time, I could finally see.

From the least to the greatest of us.

All people, including myself, have been lost and broken and at some point, we all have needed God's love, forgiveness and help.

We all need to forgive and to be forgiven.

What Jesus demonstrated and finished on The Cross...

This is the place, I believe we all must start.

Chapter Twenty

Clear

"Look at the birds of the air; they do not sow or reap or store away in barns, and yet your heavenly Father feeds them. Are you not much more valuable than they are?"

~ Matthew 6:26

Today at 43 years old having been sent out to do ministry 12 years ago by Reverend William Kerr, a very instrumental man in my life, who holds a Masters in Divinity and having been duly able to complete three years with The Welton Academy on a fully paid scholarship given to me by Dr. Jonathan Welton himself. I truly owe so many amazing people like Reverend William and his wife Sandi for putting up with me in my earlier days of transition, as well as both my Mother and Father for always being there for me, whenever I was making my honest attempts at it, great honor, respect and recognition. Judy Soul, my old probation officer and Al and Paul my A.A. Sponsors. The social workers and addiction counselors like George Davis, my Brother Mark, my Sister in Law Shauna, her husband Julian and my nephews

Micah and Corey. All of my friends and family, the churches, drug court, social programs and merciful judges. The Love that came through them all. *Through it all*, even the kind acts and gestures of strangers that met me along the way. The smile on the bus or the dollar that hundreds had given this pauper.

My wife Anna and her family and our three amazing kids, who all came after these turbulent years and to all who have attended our weekly Bible Studies and all who have helped and served in our thrift store here in The Chicagoland area. All the people in my life who have been passionate about Christ with me over the years. The people I would consider to be my present strong support group. Those who have walked with me, through all of my ups and downs ever since I walked out of that long, cold, valley of death that I was in.

After 37 arrests and more stories than what I could ever put in this book and after 36 years of being a Christian, my latter years have actually been a lot better than these former years I have just shared and disclosed with you here. I have literally died and been raised again.

I hope by the retelling of my story here you are able to see more clearly and contextually now, how Christ came to lead people out from that Old Covenant of Moses stuff that entailed stonings and death as a punishment for their infractions of the law, into The New Covenant Message of Christ's Love, Forgiveness and Help.

God's reconciling, mercy and grace. Christ's redeeming love that will come out after us, find us when we are lost and bring us back home to Our Father Who Art in Heaven.

If so, then my highest hope for the retelling of my past has been accomplished.

This is The Good News that I set out to teach and have based three previous chapters on in the heart of this book. To be able to get all of that old gloom and doom stuff in The Bible out of the way and behind us and to begin moving forward now into knowing deeper God's grace, his enduring mercy, his goodness, love and kindness and to receive His helping hand, The Potter's Hand, out of the muck and mire we may have found or even perhaps presently find ourselves in…

Getting here to this point together is like seeing a new day dawning and with these new lenses that I have been given, I am even seeing the scriptures in a light now that keeps growing their meaning brighter and brighter with each new passing day.

The scriptures today, have taken on a whole new meaning to me and they are now continually pointing me more and more unto Jesus Christ The Victorious One Himself and God Our Father with us, rather than angry God our punisher, floating around mad in the sky over us looking for whom he can punish for their failings.

These new lenses, proper interpretation, correct historical context and a better understanding of biblical times and culture along with my own personal experience with The Love of Christ just keeps making everything about my Bible and my God that much more awesome.

More Awesome than I could have ever even imagined.

Studying and understanding my Bible clearer, reading and listening to some amazing modern authors like Bill Johnson, Kris Vallotton, Greg Boyd, Harold Eberle, Alan Hawkins, N.T. Wright and so many more is like seeing all the rough places in Christ's story being made smooth again. It's like watching the moon going down with all the wreckage and confusion that bad theology brought me in the past and seeing a new day being born as the sun rises now and I am free to come into the light and knowledge of the glorious New Man and New Creation that God desires for me to be without all that former hesitance, guilt or shame that bad religion once tried to bury me in.

My identity as A Child of God has been affirmed and embraced and this to me is True New Covenant Theology. The equipping of the saints to be able to demolish all the lies we have heard from anyone about God Our Father and to finally speak the truth in love to all, until all know Christ's endless reaching love for us all.

One of my favorite verses in all The Bible comes from the beatitudes when Jesus is teaching his disciples to "Be perfect" like their Father in Heaven is perfect. As a child, I used to believe that this statement or command from Jesus to "Be perfect" was a call to personal holiness or perfect adherence to some man made set of religious rules.

I thought it was a call into the ongoing war I would have to fight against my own flesh and all the evil temptations that would continually surround and contend with me. So I developed an internal relationship with "a lie" that kept me at war with myself and just about everyone and everything around me. I would struggle with this for many years and I was in this battle that I could just never seem to win.

I would try really hard and inevitably fail time and time again.

As Paul in Romans Chapter 7 verse 15 so perfectly stated;

"I don't really understand myself, for I want to do what is right, but I don't do it. Instead, I keep doing what I hate."

Like Paul expressed here, it just always seemed like no matter how hard I would try to stay on track, I would still always fall short of perfect. I was always continually "Missing The Mark" and thus fearing God's Eternal Wrath and heavy handed punishment as a result.

In my eyes today, it's The Enemies of The Cross who teach such nonsense. The True Good News is God's love and forgiveness toward you, even when you have fallen. His compassion and willingness to correct you, heal you and to raise you up again, free from your past and to then give you a permanent position and future in His Kingdom…

Listen, even when we have not been perfect.

We are still perfectly loved by God.

As a child I saw the words of Jesus that were imploring me to "Be perfect" from Matthew Chapter 5 wrong.

As a grown man now, at 43 years old and after Christ's lifelong pursuit of me, so that I could know The Father and His patient, long-suffering love for me, I now see that same scripture in a whole new light.

Not as a standard or high bar in which none of us can jump or live up to but rather as Christ's teaching on how important it is for us all to love and be good to each other.

In conclusion, let's take a look at it together.

Jesus starts by saying;

"You have heard the law that says, 'Love your neighbor' and hate your enemy. But I say, love your enemies! Pray for those who persecute you! In that way, you will be acting as true children of your Father in heaven. For he gives his sunlight to both the evil and the good, and he sends rain on the just and the unjust alike."

~ Matthew 5:43-45

So beautiful was this revealing to me. As beautiful as the revealing I had received as a child that day when I wrote on my mom's swing. I had realized during a sunrise at 12 years old that it was not destined by God to hurt us. An amazingly freeing revelation it was to me that it was not The Father's Heart and Will that any of us should perish. A truth, I almost lost sight of in my darkest hour. What a beautiful truth and yet how easily this can be missed by our own mere position and time.

Missing it by position. If you are in a house behind walls and closed blinds you will not be able to see the sun and ever know and experience the warmth of this miracle that takes place every morning.

Sometimes, I compare the positions we take on certain things, like a theological stance or faulty political belief to an empty house with closed blinds. When we have subscribed to something despite overwhelming evidence to prove our stance wrong and yet we stubbornly refuse to face the truth and hold our pride filled ground, it's like a person sitting in darkness refusing to open the blinds.

Jesus goes on further correcting them and explaining to them that to be "True Children of God Our Father in

Heaven" we must be like Him who causes the sun to shine and the rain to fall on us all.

This is God's unceasing light, warmth, love and provision that graces the planet and all of us on it.

The good, the bad and the ugly.

He then goes on further and tells them;

"If you are kind only to your friends, how are you different from anyone else? Even pagans do that. But you are to be perfect, even as your Father in heaven is perfect."
~ Matthew 5:47-48.

If we have taken the position to remain closed minded and not open to anything other than what we have already been told and have heard by others, then we will never be able to hear anything new that God may be wanting to speak to us right now. If you remain closed minded like that house with closed blinds, you will miss seeing the sunrise due to the position you have taken.

Likewise, If you were to get up at midnight and go outside of the house into the moon's mere reflection of the descending sun's warmth and light expecting to experience the glory of the sun, I'm sorry to say that you just aren't going to see it and feel it because now your timing is a bit off.

Better positioning but just at the wrong time.

You see, I believe it's in the dawn of God's enduring love and compassion for us all that true glory, power and miracles become possible, felt, seen and experienced...

After my last release from jail, I met a small group of local drinkers who I came to love and that I used to go out and drink socially with and the joke I like to tell is that it was with these guys that I drank myself sober but gone were the days of stealing and mainlining heroin. It was finished. It was done.

I remember in this transitional time in my life that I was also getting up before dawn every morning and taking my bible and acoustic guitar up to the park by my mom's apartment in Burbank IL. to feed and sing to a whole bunch of rabbits. As I read The Bible and prayed and worshipped God in the mornings, even my desire for alcohol diminished as well...

Before I knew it, I was clean of all substances.

With hardly any effort on my part at all, it was like I was gently being unshackled and simply set free.

The miracle was happening for me.

I was being embraced by God and I knew now without any doubt that when we put our Faith in Jesus all things truly become possible.

So as I have set out with this book to unveil this message, this message of God's enduring love and mercy for us all, even the worst and most broken of us, the truth be told is that I am a nobody or at least anybody of any real significance, prominence or recognition. Yet the beauty in being a nobody, I have found is that there is truly nobody like me. Just like there is nobody like you. No story and testimony like mine, just as there is none like your own. I am an original just like you seeking to come from a genuine, pure and honest place and as you can see, I have been far from perfect in this life but *Through It All* God has continued to be very faithful and good to me, just as I am believing He has been to you.

So there it is. At least the hardest part of my story to tell.

It has actually taken me 6 years from the time I set out to write this book to be able to get all of that above down here on paper. What I hope was an easy and enjoyable read for you, was a very difficult and painful task for me. Yet, very rewarding to say the least.

I was born into a broken home and I lived as an addict on The Westside of Chicago for about a decade. I was a white kid in an all black neighborhood. I was an addict submerged in much of that community's poverty and as well spent many months in and out of Cook County lockup surrounded by gangs, drugs, shakedowns, death and unnecessary violence.

By the time I was 25 years old, I had acquired 37 arrests and had experienced more people dying than what I was able to count or barely emotionally acknowledge.

Those years have given me a lens that was hard earned and can't be undone. I can't undo what I have lived and seen. I can't be undone of these experiences. My only hope is that my retelling of these days can be of some help and insight to others.

If this story of mine can help even one person, then perhaps all of the pain that I have endured could somehow be worth something.

I hope it is at least worth the price of this book.

To be up in the middle or upper class (financially speaking) looking down on the lower class is one thing but to be at the bottom (dirt poor) looking up through what seems to be like an unbreakable glass ceiling at others succeeding and doing well is another.

Both social classes may have valid, vantage points, views and lessons to be learned from. In all actuality, I have found that it's not always the amount of income that one makes that places anyone (morally) any higher or lower on the totem pole than anyone else. I have met genuinely beautiful broke people as well as wealthy bigots. On the other hand, I have known selfish, greedy, uncaring poor people and those of more economic security who have shown themselves to be very kind and giving.

Through it all though, these roads I have taken whether chosen or drugged. These paths either on purpose with intent or just wandering around lost. I have been blessed to spend seasons with many groups of diversified cultures and people. This includes people of many differing political and religious belief systems as well and whether I have been up or down, bound or free, I have come to find that the ground at the foot of The Cross, anywhere for anyone, still truly remains on equal ground. The Forgiveness that Christ offered on The Cross is still being offered for us all. So come all and come now. Know that the Lord is good and let's experience together, in fullness, all He has done, all He is doing, and all He is still willing to do...

As we are coming to a close and landing this thing here, let me tell you that I have had some accomplishments and many more stories that I can tell you about my life after those hard pressed years. Testimonies about our successes for The Kingdom of God since those dark days out there lost in that Chicago concrete wilderness. Stories about how my relationship with both my Mother and Father are better today than it has ever been and how much better my emotional, spiritual and physical well being are. I have just as many stories about the saving grace that was sent to me in the form of my loving wife Ania and our three amazing children, Joshua, Natalie and Caleb and my testimony about a cure for Hepatitis C being found, God's providence and my system being cleared and cured of a disease that they told me for 20 years was incurable.

I can tell you beautiful stories about overcoming clinical depression and my family worshipping together and my wife and I founding and overseeing a Christian Ministry here in Chicago and about all of the providential grace, miracles and acts of kindness we have experienced from The Heart of God, ever since we decided to pursue His call on our life together as a family.

It's been a good amount of years since my days as an addict roaming the streets of Chicago and the last 16 years of my life as a faithful Husband and Father, fully given and committed to my family and our ministry is a whole other book I could and would love to write next...

So, in conclusion of this book, let me just begin that next story here.

Three years after my Awakening on the lakefront in Chicago, I met the most beautiful woman my eyes had ever seen. My prayers for years to meet a woman who believed in God as passionately as I did were answered and she walked into my life and sat down right next to me at a place I had just recently started working at.

She was from Poland and from the first time we met, we became very close and even though I tried everything to convince her that I was not a good guy for her to get involved with, she continued to pursue me. I even tried to introduce her to another friend of mine who didn't have the kind of past that I had because I could see what a beautiful and amazing girl she was and I really didn't want her to have to suffer the mess of a man that I'd become.

She has the most beautiful eyes and loving heart I have ever seen though and one night early on in our friendship, I remember telling her everything. I confessed even things that I decided not to disclose in this book. I told her the worst of the worst about me, thinking assuredly she would know better now, to just walk away.

I'll never forget it. When I was done telling her what a horrible human being I was and how wrong I had been... She said to me, "Yeah but that was who you were, that's not who you are today."

She herself had come to America and overstayed her visa. I was a 2 time felon from Chicago with 37 arrests in my background. When we met, I was 27 and she was 23. We fell in love with nothing to our names but love and faith and 16 years later, with 3 amazing kids, I'm sitting here in Poland right now writing the last chapter of this book.

Ania, my beautiful wife came to The United States when she was only 19 years old. She was born 1 of 8 siblings and ever since she came to The United States she had always dreamed of being able to go back and see her family again.

Unlike my dad who left the home when I was 7, my wife's dad was killed in a tragic tractor accident when she was only 8 years old leaving behind her Mother, 4 daughters and 3 sons.

Ania came to me and became my wife in the states. She married me and gave us three children of our own. Over the last 16 years, she has given me the healthy family and home I had always prayed, hoped and dreamed to have. So now, the dream for me had become to see her reunited home to her own family back in Poland.

Every year since our first child was born, we wanted to make this happen but shortly after Josh came, we then had Natalie and then Caleb. Work was constant but unsteady and not enough pay to be able to afford a trip like this for all five of us.

I used to tell Ania that we could send her and maybe one kid at a time each year but she would always say "No", she wasn't going to go back home until we all could go as a family. She's an amazing, committed, faithful Wife and Mother.

With all of the unsteady work and layoffs and jobs that paid the bills but not much more than that, we just never seemed like we could get up enough money to afford a trip like this. So about five years ago, we finally took a leap of faith and stepped out into self employment together and since then, with the help of God, some really amazing clients and good people in our lives, we have been able to make this dream trip of ours come true. As a matter of fact, after many years of being a resident just last month before taking this trip she as well became an official sworn in Citizen of The United States of America.

Even more amazingly, our trip here has been to Ania's youngest siblings wedding, so everyone in her family, even her brother from Scotland and a brother in law from Germany and her only sister back home from the states have all been able to make this trip. It has taken her 19 years total and today as I sit here and write this, she is here in Poland with all of her siblings and her mom again.

God is so Good!

As a matter of fact, I'm at her mom's house with my oldest son Josh, while Ania is at the beach in Maniowy Poland with her brother, his wife and our daughter Natalie and our youngest son Caleb.

You see, this is the continued story of a young broken man from Chicago wanting a healthy family and home of his own so bad and a young woman from Poland giving him one and wanting to see her own healthy family back in Poland again and this man from Chicago doing all he can to make this happen.

Only God could have written this story.

Whew! Deep Breath.

So now, with my darker, former years thoroughly confessed and disclosed, it is my hope that I can move on and begin to tell you more about the better and latter years. The stuff after the storm.

Thank You sincerely from my heart for listening.

I hope we both may have found something in all of this together that could increase our shared faith and love for God, family, ourselves and one another.

I have been praying the whole time I have been writing;

"That Christ may dwell in your hearts through faith. And I pray that you, being rooted and grounded in love, may have power, together with all the saints, to comprehend the length and width and height and depth of His love, and to know the love of Christ that surpasses knowledge, that you may be filled with all the fullness of God ..."

~ Ephesians 3:17-19

My life as a broken kid, grieving his parents' breakup and those years wandering around out there medicating neglect, abandonment, abuse and depression with street drugs, hasn't been a real easy one to get through, to say the least but my hope is that many will see that if God could take and use a broken guy like me, baggage and all...

Then there has to be more than enough hope for anyone.

Whoever you are, wherever you are, you are not too far.

You're actually a lot closer than you think.

Christ's Spirit, Our Comforter and Our Helper is always as near as the air we breathe and the next few words we speak.

It is my hope that I can now get on with writing books for the strengthening, comfort, and edification of The Body of Christ.

"The beginning of wisdom is this: Get wisdom. Though it cost all you have."

~ Proverbs 4:7

Regardless of who you are, where you were born, the color of your skin, what you have or don't have, what you have done, or haven't...

"Our Father who Art In Heaven"
~ Matthew 6:9

"Your Redeemer who formed you in your mother's womb" ~ Isaiah 44:24

I don't believe The Creator and maker of all things in Heaven and Earth has ever destined us to be hurt, neglected or forsaken. These are things we sadly do to one another, as human beings not living and remaining in an awareness of His love and concern for us all.

I personally believe God likes to see us all faithfully helping and getting along with one another as any Father likes to see his kids playing and getting along with each other and as a lifelong seeker of truth and hearer of many differing views, knowing that some of what I have set out to say in this book could be a bit controversial or even contended with I have always felt it the respectful and kind thing to do as a Christian to just try and remain a good calm listener.

Even when I disagree, I always try to respond with words that will be gracious and redemptive, rather than hurtful or mean.

As well, if I was to be called out into a debate that ended up going that way, hurtful and mean, I just as well would rather let you have your win for the day and stay fixed and rooted in the love and peace that God has placed in my heart. I often value peace over my need to prove I'm right. So even in all I have sought to teach in this book, one thing I do know for sure.

For a man who has lived my life on the outside, I too have experienced the loving redeeming hand of God extended through Jesus Christ the son and have experienced an ongoing relationship with Him...

Through it all.

And The Good News of Christ and His Kingdom is truly A Message for us all. The good, the bad and the ugly.

"You search the Scriptures because you think they give you eternal life. But the Scriptures point to me! Yet you refuse to come to me to receive this." ~ Matthew 5:39-40

"I am the way and the truth and the life. No one comes to the Father except through me." ~ John 14:6

At this time more than anything, I would love for us all to acknowledge Jesus together and give him thanks for all the good things he has continually brought to us and to Thank Him for all he has brought us through and to Thank Him for all that is still yet to come...

In His Unfailing Love and Name.

Thank You Jesus!

"When they came to the place called The Skull, they crucified Him there, along with the criminals, one on His right and the other on His left."

Then Jesus Said,

"Father, forgive them, for they do not know what they are doing"
~ Luke 23:34

To be continued…

Stay in Love,

thepotterschurch.com

All scriptures taken from either an N.I.V. or the N.L.T bible

Some names have been changed to protect the identity of certain individuals who would not want to be associated with this story.

Made in the USA
Monee, IL
21 May 2021